POSITIVE AFFIRMATIONS
For Black Women

365 Days of Inspiration for Contemporary Black Women and BIPOCs: Each day Reprogram Your Thoughts, Develop Confidence and Love for Yourself, and Attract Success.

By

Imani Williams

The Way to Success Consulting LLC Editions

The Way to Success Consulting LLC Editions

Table of Contents

Introduction

Even though there are a lot of ways to take care of yourself, one of the most beneficial things you can do is get into the habit of saying positive things to yourself first thing in the morning. It has been demonstrated that your mental condition has a more direct influence on your behavior than your physical state does. This refers to both the things that you do and the things that you choose not to do. As someone who has struggled with anxiety in the past, I well understand how difficult this can be. At some point in our lives, every one of us reaches a point where we decide that we no longer choose to be governed by negativity, whether it comes from within ourselves or from the outside world. Affirmations in the morning are an excellent tool for achieving this goal.

Affirmations first thing in the morning are a helpful tool for building and restoring confidence in black women, who frequently have to navigate the intersection of race and gender. We are frequently complimented on our "strength," despite the fact that we have unhealthy attachments to things and people that do not serve our best interests. Because of the potential for this to become exhausting, we need words of encouragement to boost not only ourselves but also one another. My identity as a black woman has made it difficult for me to fully appreciate who I am, and I have far too often made the mistake of contrasting myself with other people. Finally, I'm getting to the point where I'm learning to accept every aspect of myself, including my skin tone, hair, physique, and freckles.

I've put together a list of morning affirmations for black women that you may recite to yourself first thing in the morning to get your thoughts organized and keep a positive attitude throughout the day. Because having a thankful attitude and affirming oneself go hand in hand, you may come across a few affirmation quotes that will help you practice gratitude first thing in the morning. This is because having a grateful attitude and affirming oneself go hand in hand.

I have high hopes that after reading these morning affirmations, you will feel confident, gorgeous, witty, driven, and ready to take on anything that life throws at you.

Month January, Chapter 1

January 1

> You are wonderful and brilliant.

A long time ago, I concluded that I required my very own slogan. I came up with the phrase "you are beautifully and wonderfully made" based on the phrase "you are fearfully and wonderfully fashioned" found in the Bible as something specific and significant that I could say to myself in order to treat myself with care and comfort while simultaneously firmly rooting myself in the here and now. This is something I constantly remind myself of, and it is something that actually helps me find peace in the knowledge that I am perfect just the way I am and that I don't require anything additional other than what is already present within me.

Make coming up with a memorable motto for yourself your resolution for the new year. Repeat that to yourself as you look in the mirror on a daily basis.

January 2

> The destination is never the place itself, but rather a shift in perspective on how things are seen.

In recent years, I've been incredibly blessed with the opportunity to embark on a significant amount of travel. While I was traveling, I saw one of the most important things to me, and that was how much we take for granted. I've been to slums where residents walk around barefoot and unprotected from the bitter cold by wearing neither shoes nor coats. I've been to places where people labor really hard at occupations that are both physically and mentally taxing for a very little wage. It instilled in me the value of each and every person on the planet, as well as the importance of never taking my work for granted.

The objective is to maintain an open mind toward everything and to devote at least one day (or week) to discovering a new part of the world. If you are unable to afford to take time off from work, consider traveling to a new part of the city you already live in. Give thanks for everything you already possess.

January 3

> There is a meaning to every aspect of existence. If you share your experience, you may end up assisting another person in finding their own.

Because the difficulties I've encountered are still taboo to talk about, I made the decision to talk openly about my personal experiences anyway. Self-harm, eating disorders, addiction, and mental health issues are topics that are rarely broached in an open forum. However, it is of the utmost importance that somebody starts talking about these issues in order to make people who are suffering aware that there is support available to them. For the young woman who does not currently possess any, it is my duty to shine a light of hope in her life.

Objective: To advocate for people who are unable to do so at this time. Lend them your help and the power of your support.

January 4

> There may be times in life when you are faced with difficulties, but it will be well worth it if you are able to push through them. It is preferable to experience the full range of human emotions rather than none at all.

When I was at the funeral for my father, this phrase came to mind, and it was quite helpful in getting me through the trauma. I felt like I was riding a roller coaster of emotions. I used to drink or put restrictions on myself in an attempt to numb the severe pain that I was going through at the time. It is not uncommon for people to turn to painkillers in order to ease the pain they are experiencing; yet, it takes much more courage to go through the fire with your eyes open. I decided against using medicines to dull the pain I was in and instead gave myself permission to feel every emotion that came to the surface. My life was going through a challenging time, yet allowing myself to feel loss and despair helped pave the path for the celebration of his life that was to come later. It made it possible for me to start the healing process in a way that was both healthy and honest.

Your mission is to give yourself permission to experience the one sensation you've been trying to avoid feeling. Make a call to a close friend, open up to them, and discuss it with them.

January 5

> Our planet is home to an incredible variety of wonderful and dazzling creatures. You should not let anything prevent you from reaching your full potential.

There have been many people in my life who have told me that I am incapable of achieving anything. You are being evaluated by those persons, and you must not give in to their attempts to bring you down. True friends will encourage and support you. Because no one else will believe in you if you don't, you shouldn't listen to anyone who tries to convince you that you can't make your dream a reality.

The objective is to pick one thing that you've been putting off and begin working on it right away. Don't be afraid.

January 6

> Face your deepest, most crippling fear; once you do, that fear will no longer hold any sway over you.

As a child, I had a terrible fear of throwing up, which contributed to the development of my bulimia. I was unconsciously reenacting the dread that I hold most dear. I hated throwing up so much that I actually caused it to happen to myself.

Your goal should be to learn to let go of your worries rather than let them control your life. Keep in mind that every challenge and opportunity that presents itself in your life has a certain function.

The Seventh of January

> If you change the way that you think, you will change your life.

When I was battling with depression, I remember hearing this sentence and at first being unable to fathom what it meant for me. After deciding to put what I had learned into action, I discovered a whole new realm of possibilities. Replace your positive, self-affirming thoughts with your negative, self-deprecating thoughts. When you have a positive outlook on both yourself and the world around you, you begin to see things from a different perspective. The way you live your life right now is entirely up to you.

The objective is to be conscious of the tenor of your views.

January 8

> There is nothing more important than love.

There have been many times in my life when I have felt as though I had no direction or purpose, but whenever I focus on the love I have in my heart, not only for my friends and family but also for my own life, I am able to find a sense of calm and contentment.

Your mission is to let everyone know that you adore them. Raise as much of a ruckus as you can about it; bake them a cake; write them a letter; or draw them a picture. When you have so much to offer, don't give them the opportunity to take your love for granted.

January 9

Go where you're needed and stay away from where you're not. Put yourself in situations and with people that will boost your mood.

Spend as little time as possible with people who don't value or appreciate you for who you are and what you bring to the table. There are a lot of women that I know who continue to pursue men in the expectation that they can change them, or I have friends who don't have their best interests at heart, but unfortunately, that strategy does not work. A healthy amount of respect for each other is one of the most important parts of lasting friendships and partnerships.

Your objective is to not squander your time by following behind the people who have told you that they do not want you around. Evaluate all of your connections and get rid of the ones that aren't working out for you.

The Tenth of January

Don't discount your emotions. Don't forget about them.

When my feelings were particularly nasty, painful, or uncomfortable, I would flee and hide from them. I used to do it all the time. But as time has gone on, I've come to realize that it's okay to accept every one of my feelings. I am aware that in order for me to move past them, the first step is for me to acknowledge and accept all of my sentiments. They are ingrained in my very being. As a direct consequence of this, they are authentic and carry significant meaning.

Pick a feeling that makes you uncomfortable, whether it's because it's embarrassing or frightening. It is okay to experience emotions such as fear, fury, or grief as long as you do not let those feelings define who you are. Recognize and accept your emotions, and keep in mind how important they are.

The Eleventh of January

> You have a lot of smarts in your head. You have both of your feet inside your shoes. You are the master of your own fate and can do anything you set your mind to.

This is your life, and you have everything you need to live the life you've always dreamed of right here within you. Construct your own reality by drawing on what you've learned and the experiences you've had. The amazing thing about life is that if you don't like where you are, there is always a new moment and a new day to start over. If you don't like where you are, there is always a chance to start over.

Make informed conclusions. Inspire yourself to make choices in the now that will lead to the future you want.

The 12th of January

> A dream is an aspiration that originates in your heart.

Even though it may appear to be simple, this is actually one of the most profound lessons that any of the Disney fairy tales have ever imparted to us. We have the ability to become anyone we want to be and go wherever we want to go when we grow up. If you have a goal, you should make every effort to pursue it with your whole heart. It is possible to imagine anything.

Make a wish with all of your heart, and work hard to achieve every goal you set for yourself.

You, and only you, have the power to do what you set out to do. Nobody else can complete the task for you.

The 13th of January

> If you change the way you think, your life will change as a result.

When I was struggling with depression, I remember hearing this sentence and at first being unable to fathom what it meant. When I finally decided to put it into action, it was like walking into a completely new universe for me. Good, encouraging thoughts about oneself should replace negative, self-deprecating thoughts. When you have confidence in yourself and in the people and things around you, you start to see the world in a different way. Everything that happens in your life right now is up to you.

Aim: Pay careful attention to the flavor of your thoughts.

January 14

> There is nothing more important than love.

This short lyric contains a great deal of truth. Above all, love makes everything better. Throughout my life, I have often felt lost and without hope. However, if I focus on the love I have in my heart, not only for my friends and family but also for my own life, I am able to feel at peace.

The goal is to make it clear to everyone who is important to you. Create a picture for them, bake them a cake, send them a letter, or shout it from the rooftops to get their attention. When you have so much to offer, you shouldn't give them the opportunity to take advantage of your affection.

The 15th of January

> Go where you are wanted and avoid where you are not. Put yourself in situations and with people that will make you happy.

You should limit the amount of time you spend with those who cannot see or appreciate what you have to offer. I know a lot of women who keep pursuing men with the aim of changing them or friends who don't have their best interests at heart, but it never works out for them. I also know a lot of people who don't have their best interests at heart. Respect for each other is one of the most important parts of lasting friendships and partnerships.

The objective is to avoid wasting time trying to track down people who have made it clear they do not want you in their lives. Examine each of your associations and cut ties with those that aren't beneficial.

The 16th of January

> Don't discount your emotions. Pay attention to what they say.

In the past, whenever my feelings were upsetting, painful, or otherwise uncomfortable, I would try to escape and hide from them. But as time has gone on, I've come to realize that it's okay to accept every one of my feelings. I am aware that in order to move past them, the first step is for me to identify and embrace every feeling that I am experiencing. They are an essential component of my identity. Because of this, they are deserving of significance and legitimacy.

Pick a feeling that makes you uncomfortable, whether it's because it's embarrassing or frightening. It's okay to feel things like fear, fury, or grief as long as you don't let those feelings define who you are. Recognize and accept your emotions, and remind yourself of the value they hold.

The 17th of January

> You've got brains in your mind. You are walking around with your feet in your shoes. You have complete control over your future.

This is your life, and you already own everything you require to live the life you've always dreamed of right here, right now. Make use of what you've encountered and learned to create the world that you want for yourself. The amazing thing about life is that if you don't like where you are, there's always a new moment and a new day to start over again. If you don't like where you are, there's always a chance to start over.

The objective is to form well-informed opinions. Convince yourself that the decisions you want to make for your future can be made right now.

The 18th of January

> Create the best possible relationship with yourself.

Over the course of my life, I've been forced to become my own closest friend by necessity. I was miserable and isolated throughout the majority of my heartbreaks, and I spent many hours crying myself to sleep. I understood that in order to triumph over the misery, I would have to train myself to console and comfort myself. Even though it's a process, and even though I'm continually improving my skills, I've come a long way. I have a firm conviction that I am my own closest companion.

The objective is to love oneself and to behave toward oneself in the same way that one would behave toward a close friend. You have earned the right to be loved in the same manner in which you love the people around you.

The 19th of January

> It is less important what a person is born with than who they become as they get older.

Everyone's story starts out differently because we all come from different places. Our lives all get off to different starts, but when we put our minds and bodies into something that we are truly enthusiastic about, there is no obstacle that can stand in our way. Your reward and level of success will depend on how hard you work and how well your work pays off.

Aim to be proud of who you are as well as where you came from. Imagine yourself in the future, both in terms of where you want to go and who you want to become.

20th of The Month

> My mother advised me that if I couldn't find anything to live for, I should at least find something to die for.

On this beautiful planet, we each have a unique purpose. It is up to each of us to mold our lives and decide how we want to go about living them. The most important thing is to have a cause that you are passionate about and that connects you to the direction you want to take your life in.

Find something in life that excites you enough to get out of bed every morning and commit to accomplishing that thing. That's the goal. Take a stand for the things you believe in.

January 21

> When your feet start to hurt, try to imagine what it's like for someone else who has the same problem.

It is far too simple to become preoccupied with one's own life and allow oneself to be overcome by misfortune as a result. It is frequently impossible to detect that you are engaging in the activity since you are so engrossed in it. This is dangerous because you run the risk of becoming detached from the real world. Remember that there is always someone who has it much worse than you do, but don't let that make you ignore your feelings or your problems.

The goal is to broaden one's perspective through engaging in philanthropic work or community service. Create a list of 10–15 things or people that you are glad for, regardless of how insignificant or significant they might appear to be.

The 22nd of January

> When your feet start to hurt, try to imagine what it's like for someone else who has the same problem.

People in this world will use you for their own gain and give you feedback based on their perceptions of who you are. It is up to you to decide how you will use that information. If you give other people the power to make decisions for you, you are giving up your dignity. However, if you can remember to connect with your higher power, you will always have a chance to regain it.

The objective is to not give someone the opportunity to take advantage of you or manipulate you.

The 23rd of January

> Remind yourself that you are deserving of the love and the life that you want and that you have the right to have both.

In my perspective, everything that happens for a specific reason.

In my perspective, there is no such thing as a coincidence. In my opinion, things unfold in the manner in which they should. If you look back over your life and study every experience you've had, you'll notice that each one was a direct result of anything you did or thought.

The goal is to not fight against or try to avoid unplanned occurrences. Your life will, over time and in its own unique way, become better because of it in some way.

The 24th of January

> The belief that one does not own sufficient power is the most common reason people give away their power.

You are showing a sign of weakness if you give in to other people's demands and enable them to put you down and tell you that you have nothing to contribute. By submitting, you are in effect giving them permission to use your information. Nobody has the authority to take away your power; it is solely in your control and cannot be exercised by anyone else.

The goal is for you to make effective use of the voice that has been provided to you. Raise your voice as loudly as you can for the things in which you have faith. Never give anyone the power to make you stop speaking.

The 25th of January

> You are the only person who knows what is best for you, so you should trust your gut instincts.

Pay as much attention to your intuition as you would to the advice of a doting parent or a trusted companion. This is the most genuine part of your soul, and it is the location of the key that unlocks the door to your happiness. At other times, the noise of our own thoughts, our worries, or the voices of others might become deafening. You should do everything that is necessary in order to rejoin.

Today's task: Pay attention to what your gut is telling you.

The 26th of January

> It is not the melancholy of tomorrow that is diminished by worry; rather, it is the power of the present moment.

It's possible that there are some people who believe that worrying has a purpose in their lives. Whatever you're working on, worrying about it will sap all of your energy and passion for it. It's in our nature to be anxious, but when we let it consume us on a consistent basis, we invite more problems into our lives. It will provide you with something to do, but you won't make any progress by doing it.

Aim: When you find yourself feeling anxious about anything in the future, keep in mind that you do not always have control of the situation. Instead, you should focus on something useful, such as creating a schedule or a budget. Take the initiative and relax rather than clenching your teeth. In the end, it won't make a difference in the outcome.

The 27th of January

> Never be ashamed or embarrassed about your feelings. You have the right to experience any feeling that strikes your fancy and to engage in any activity that brings you pleasure.

We are not just automatons. Our capacity to simultaneously feel a diverse variety of emotions is a defining characteristic of what it means to be human. In spite of the fact that it might, at times, feel overwhelming, the human body is nevertheless rather remarkable. I have both laughed because I was crying and cried because I was laughing. In any case, showing your feelings is not a sign of weakness, but of strength and ambition.

Watching a hilarious movie or listening to a sorrowful song is the objective of this activity. Recognize and embrace your emotions, and take pride in them.

The 28th of January

> It's better to be fully ridiculous than completely boring, and it's better to be completely ridiculous than completely dull. Imperfections are beautiful, and madness is magnificent.

I didn't suspect I had bipolar disorder until I started going to therapy. There, I learned that bipolar disorder is a condition that is diagnosed and treated by psychiatrists. Because it is not something I can control, I had no choice but to seek counseling for it, and I am not ashamed of having done so. When you take into consideration that each of us is dealing with our own unique difficulties, you concluded that we need to come together as a community in order to aid and support one another. These problems can be as small as a spot or as big as a mental illness.

The goal is to always act politely and seek assistance for oneself or a friend's problems, regardless of how insignificant the circumstance may appear to be. Take a look at this page for some helpful resources.

The 29th of January

> Our secrets sicken us.

It's common for us to be oblivious to the fact that the things we keep to ourselves can be rather detrimental. I had to come to terms with the fact that the fact that I was harboring things inside of me was one of the primary reasons I wanted to use alcohol and drugs in the first place—to run away from myself. Once I allowed myself to feel, I was able to start the healing process. By sharing how I've been feeling with another person and having a conversation about it, I'm able to shake off the weight of the emotion that's been suffocating me.

A close friend or member of your family should be informed about something you've been keeping a secret from them. Note how much better you feel when you've completed the task.

The 30th of January

> Make it your goal, rather than your success, to be of value to others.

It is far too simple to avoid becoming sidetracked by the quest for success, wealth, and celebrity status. If that is the kind of acknowledgment that you seek in life, you will be disappointed because it is not genuine and it will not last. We are here to help people in our own special ways, to bring value to them, and to act as a resource for them. We are not the same thing as our achievements. Simply put, it serves as a timely reminder of our capabilities.

The goal is to think about what is essential to you and to make sure that you are acting for the right reasons and not just to satisfy your own ego. Check to see if the goals you have set for yourself are beneficial to you.

January 31st

> Just give it your all, and afterward, when you need a break, sing a song to yourself.

There are moments when the only option you have is to give it your absolute best effort. Make sure you give yourself the time you need to focus on yourself and find something that brings you joy. Singing is my passion. Singing or performing music allows me to forget about whatever is upsetting me and move on with my life. If sports are your passion, then you should get outside and play! If you're pushing yourself too hard, take some time out for some yoga or meditation. Finding ourselves is the most important thing that can be done.

Singing aloud should be today's priority. Create a fool out of yourself by laughing and dancing inappropriately. Give yourself permission to take pleasure in whatever brings you happiness. You are deserving of it!

Month February, Chapter 2

1st of February

> When we show the world that we love it, it opens its arms to us.

What you put out into the world will come back to you in some form. When you give off positive energy, you will attract more of the same in return. It is quite astounding how the power of love can bring serenity to any situation. Even if other people behave in a way that is harmful or poisonous, a response filled with love and compassion can be quite effective. You know that you will be able to sleep comfortably at night regardless of the outcome because you are confident that you did the right thing, which is the only thing you can control.

Today, show the world how much love you have within you by wearing your emotions on your sleeve like a badge of honor. You should try to give as many people a hug as you can, or you should try to make as many people happy as you can.

The Second of February

> If your heart is truly set on something, no request is too absurd to make.

The only thing that really matters is that you do things that you enjoy. There is no such thing as an impossible ideal, so long as it caters to your most heartfelt desires. In point of fact, the more ambitious your goals are, the more joy you'll attract into your life.

The goal of today is to give yourself permission to dream big and to find peace in the knowledge that just thinking about your goals puts you one step closer to actually achieving them.

The Third of February

My only piece of advice is to keep an eye out, listen carefully, and yell for help if you need it.

Carry on transforming yourself, expanding your horizons, learning from your mistakes, falling in love, having your heart broken, and then doing it all over again. Everything that happens to us helps us become more alive, vivid, and joyful as we go through it. You should not let feelings of fear or humiliation prevent you from moving forward. Continue on and keep living.

Confronting one of your fears should be today's primary focus. Try to think back on a trying event you've had in the past and what you took from it. In what ways did it facilitate your growth?

4th of February

If there is no answer to an issue, the problem will never be resolved. Better sooner than later!

I make it a point to start each day by engaging in the activities that give me the greatest cause for concern; doing so helps me feel both more robust and more capable as the day progresses. When our worries and worries have been taken care of, we can move on to more important things.

No matter what happens, the goal for today is to tie up all of the loose ends that remain. I can guarantee that you will experience a significant improvement in how you feel today and possibly for the rest of the week as well.

February 5

> It's possible that you'll be sad all through the night, but you'll feel better in the morning.

There are moments when we have to shed tears in order to experience true joy. When things are difficult, you should let yourself feel the grief that you are experiencing. Let your tears fall freely, knowing that they won't last forever and that you have something wonderful coming your way soon.

If you find yourself feeling upset, your goal should be to remind yourself of the pleasure that will undoubtedly follow. Always remember that the night will be the darkest before the morning.

The date is February 6th.

> Some people find that scars, similar to war wounds, have a certain allure. They illustrate what you've been through and how tough you are in the face of hardship by demonstrating what you've gone through.

Scars are visible evidence that a person has been through a painful experience. Some of us have physical scars that serve as a constant reminder of the challenging journeys we have traveled. The battles we've fought and won have left many of us with hidden wounds that serve as metaphors for the ordeals we've endured.

Consider your wounds and how they have shaped your life in positive ways. This is the goal.

Once you've mastered how to communicate with others, there is virtually no challenge that you and your team won't be able to conquer together.

February 7.

> People will never reach consensus on anything since no two people are exactly the same.

Every one of us comes from a different background, and this plays a role in how we understand both ourselves and the world around us. When I couldn't seem to connect with someone, I used to feel really overwhelmed and irritated about it. But as time has gone on, I've realized that what's most important in human relationships is not necessarily agreeing on everything; rather, it's learning how to communicate despite our differences in opinion and perspective.

Aim: If there is something that has been upsetting you, bring it up in a kind manner with a friend or coworker. Don't try to hide how you really feel; rather, focus on finding ways that you and the other people involved can collaborate to find a solution. Describe how you are feeling as a result of the circumstance, as well as the steps you are going to take to prevent it from happening again.

The 8th of February

> Those who are willing to take the risk of overstepping their bounds are the only ones who know how far they can go.

We educate ourselves via experience by boldly and confidently pushing the limits of our capabilities. It is preferable to try, even if it is unsuccessful, rather than speculate about what may have happened. The potential outcomes might be paralyzing.

Don't hold back on the things that are essential to you; instead, test yourself to see how much of yourself you can offer and how far you can go. This is your goal. If you don't want to have regrets in the future, you should give your best effort to live the life you want right now. What steps can you take today so that tomorrow you can start living the life you've always dreamed of?

February 9

The best investment you can make is in your health.

A healthy body is something that can never be bought with any amount of money. Take care of oneself first and foremost, and always keep an attitude of gratitude. You ought to count your blessings that you were able to get up today because tomorrow is not a given. I had been so accustomed to taking for granted the health that had been bestowed upon me by God that I had forgotten how blessed I am to be alive today. Our bodies are our temples. Think of it as your safe sanctuary.

Your mission for the day is to take care of your body in some way. Take a yoga class, go for a jog, or go for a walk. First and foremost, you should be grateful for the life you have right now.

February 10th

Instead of traveling in the direction that the path might go, you should walk in the direction where there is no path and leave a trace.

Sometimes it is easier and safer to just follow in the footsteps of others. But none of the incredible advances that we've made in recent times would have been possible if we hadn't explored new territories and thought up new concepts. If Thomas Edison had not had faith in the potential of electricity, there would be no light. If Rosa Parks had not been willing to fight for what she believed in herself, she would not have been able to inspire others to do the same. We have the ability to change the world if we choose not to listen to those who tell us that we can't or that we shouldn't do something.

February 11th

> Get away from the herd and blaze your own trail; come up with something fresh.

Consider broadening the perspective from which you view the world.

The scope of what is feasible is virtually unbounded.

February 12

> The very same emotion that has the potential to break your heart can also be the force that brings it back together again.

When I'm coping with anything painful, like loss or heartbreak, I sometimes find myself spending a lot of time looking for answers to problems that I already know the answers to. I hear a million different pieces of advice on how to deal with something or someone, but I always seem to miss the most obvious aspect, which is the possibility that the very thing that is causing me agony could also be the thing that saves my life.

It is important to keep in mind that there is not always an immediate response. Exercise patience and seek the counsel of someone who has more life experience than you do.

13 February

> We all have a childlike quality about us.

When I'm feeling angry or irritated with someone, I try to bring myself back to the fact that they were once a child.

I close my eyes and try to picture how they were when they were younger, and when I open them again, the only feelings I have for that person are love and compassion. It no longer matters what happened to them that caused them to behave in the way that they do because their innocence triumphs, and I am compelled to feel humbled in their presence as a result.

See the good in everyone, even your adversaries, and have compassion for those who wrong you. Keep in mind that you can never truly know what is happening when the doors are closed. As a result of this, show sympathy toward their behavior. They are most likely suffering from the same thing themselves.

February 14th

It is best not to put things off because there will never be an ideal time.

There are times when we sit back and wait for the right opportunity to act. It has come to my attention that waiting can bring about unhappiness for us. My efforts to attain those goals ultimately led to the majority of the noteworthy occurrences that have transpired in my life. It does not suggest that something nice will never happen by chance, since it will, especially if you put in the effort and think positively. What it does imply is that something good will not happen by accident very often. However, there are times in life when we simply have to go after what we want and risk failing.

Your objective is to take the first big step toward achieving something you've been delaying.

February 15th

Travel with all of your heart, no matter where you go.

As long as we stay true to what we feel in our hearts, we will always arrive at sincere, genuine, and supportive decisions. In my opinion, there should be more people in this world who are able to guide others from the heart and love without reservation or expectation. If we all act on issues that we feel strongly about, our chances of being successful will be significantly increased.

The objective is to pay heed to your gut feelings and keep in mind that they are never wrong. Have faith in your own spirit, and show love to everyone around you.

The sixteenth of February

You cannot be considered bold if you never ask for help.

It's possible that the strain of repressing powerful feelings could do more damage than you realize when it piles up over time. The act of seeking aid is never simple, but you should try to do so whenever you need it. Send an SOS signal by either writing a message, calling someone, or taking any other action that may be required. Help is always available, and the people who are the most courageous around the globe are the ones who are able to ask for it.

Your mission is to be as brave as you can and tell someone that you need help.

February 17th

If you have good thoughts, they will shine like beams of sunshine off of your face, and as a result, others will always find you to be attractive.

Your pleasure will rub off on others when you finally take charge of your own life and happiness. When a person is joyful, they radiate an aura of attractiveness that cannot be replicated by anything else in the world. One never knows how much of a difference a friendly smile or a sincere "How are you, really?" could make in another person's day or even in their life.

The end goal is to smile and show off your beauty to the rest of the world. Be conscious of the feelings that those around you are experiencing, and keep in mind the impact that you may be having on them.

The date is February 18th.

> I'm egocentric, irritable, and unreliable. Errors I start making are out of my control and occasionally may be challenging to manage. But if you can't support me in my worst moment, then you definitely can't reward me in my best moment. In fact, you won't deserve me in my best moment if you can't support me in my worst moment.

Whoever truly cares about you and supports you will always be there for you. They will not disappoint you. The best way to figure out who your genuine friends are is to look at who stays by your side during difficult moments like these. True friends are those who are always there for you. If they are unable to accept you when you are going through a difficult time, then it is clear that they do not deserve you when you are performing at your highest level. When choosing the people, you want to be around, it is essential to keep this in mind while you make your decisions.

The objective is to make sure that you are the kind of friend that you would want in your life. Be thankful for the connections you've made, which have demonstrated the value others place on you.

February 19th

> The pursuit of beauty is essential to self-assurance. Inner tranquility is the foundation of outer beauty.

On some of the occasions I've attended, there have been stunningly attractive women who are too shy to approach anyone because they are embarrassed by their appearance. I can sense that they are anxious about this. It may be that they don't think they're attractive enough or that they don't believe they're dressed appropriately, but either way, it quickly dims the light that shines from within. Nothing is more attractive to me than a person who is not self-conscious about their physical appearance.

Figure out what puts you at ease and boosts your self-confidence. Keep in mind how special you are, and don't be afraid to display it!

February 20

> A mistake is an opportunity for us to learn, grow, and make our future better.

It's far too easy to judge ourselves harshly for mistakes we've made in the past. Making errors is an inevitable and normal element of being human and going through life. Our failures and mistakes are opportunities for us to keep on learning and developing. You shouldn't expect to never make the same mistakes again, even if you are successful in learning from them. You most certainly will, and that is fine.

Your goal is to keep moving forward and to see each challenge as an opportunity to learn something new; if you do this, you will be surprised at how easy it is to progress.

21st of February

> If God is making me go through it, then I know it's something I need to learn from and grow from.

When things are extremely challenging and unpleasant, all that is able to enter our minds is, "Why on earth do I have to go through this?" On the other hand, there is a more effective way to handle challenging circumstances in life. Instead of fighting against it, you should try to submit to it and think about the reasons why it was given to you rather than to someone else. If you are managing it, then it is something that is inherent to your journey.

Aim: Instead of focusing on the discomfort you are experiencing, search for strategies that you may practice and perfect for the next time you go through a challenging situation.

February 22nd

> When people are unable to express themselves, they break down into smaller and smaller pieces over time.

Music has always been a medium through which I can express myself in ways that words cannot. Because of my line of work, I get to use both my voice and my music to communicate with and motivate other people, which is one of the most fulfilling aspects of my profession. I know what it's like to be shut up in your room by yourself, feeling broken and injured on the inside and out, wishing to feel loved and connected to someone, and desperately wanting to be by yourself. My songs aren't just for me; they're for everyone else who feels lonely and wants someone to talk to. They are for anyone who has ever had the experience of wanting someone to support them and be there for them when they needed it. In the event that you are reading this book, I want you to know that I am here for you and that I want to help you get through the worst times in your life.

The objective is to listen to any music that lifts your mood. If you're a musician or songwriter, pick up your instrument and let your creativity flow.

February 23rd

> Some of the most stunning and exquisite things in the world cannot be seen or even touched; rather, they must be felt with the heart in order to be understood.

What makes life so wonderful are the things that cannot be seen or touched. The experiences and emotions that stand out as the most vivid in my mind are ones that cannot be adequately described or replicated. I wasted a lot of time and energy trying to get high from substances like alcohol and narcotics when, unbeknownst to me at the time, the most potent high was standing right in front of me the whole time: life.

The objective is to give yourself some time to relax and take pleasure in something amazing that you cannot see but can feel.

February 24

Never settle for being a lesser version of someone else when you can work toward becoming a superior version of yourself.

You are as unique as a snowflake, and there is no one else on the planet just like you. It is a waste of time to spend your time trying to be like someone else. Be the best possible version of yourself, and take pride in it. You reach your full potential when you are yourself, not when you are someone else. If we all looked the same, spoke the same language, and moved in the same manner, nobody would stand out. There would be no such thing as individuality. Being unique is what sets us apart from others and gives the world its charm.

The objective is to assess your individuality. Be sure that you are not copying the style of another person and are instead being true to who you are. Be eccentric since "normal" is such a dull word!

February 25

Change demands courage.

Alteration is an unavoidable component of existence, despite the fact that it might be unsettling. Change is synonymous with growth, and growth suggests that we are progressing as a whole. When I was a kid, my parents always told me that in order for me to grow up, I needed to learn certain things and acquire certain skills. As I became older, I realized that the things I needed to acquire were not only more challenging to comprehend and master, but they were also of greater significance to me. It has endowed my life with a much deeper sense of meaning. Remember to be strong, bold, and courageous while you go through your own growing pains in life, since you are developing and becoming a better person even though you are going through these growing pains. Growing requires guts.

The question is, what would you like to change about your life or about yourself?

February 26

> Find the perseverance to take things one step at a time in order to make it happen.

No matter how beautiful or terrible your life has been up to this point, you shouldn't take it for granted. Every second of our lives provides us with valuable lessons. Every one of us has a one-of-a-kind life filled with events that nobody else could possibly fully understand. If you have an experience that you would like to share with others, it should have a lot of valuable lessons that can motivate, instruct, and inspire them. During the course of therapy, I was exposed to a wide variety of patients' experiences. Simply by listening, I was able to pick up a lot of new information. I am thankful that I was able to find the courage to talk about my experience and share what I've been going through with others. Not only has it been beneficial to me, but it has also been beneficial to many other people by providing them with strength and perspective. I encourage you to proceed in the same manner.

Your mission is to share what you've learned with someone else. You never know how a single sentence from your life story might motivate someone else to rethink the story they've been telling themselves.

Sunday, February 27

> Absolutely nothing is out of the question, as the word "potential" says right there in the phrase.

The scope of what you can do in this life is determined by your level of capability. Our knowledge and consciousness continue to expand, and as a result, things that we previously considered impossible are suddenly becoming imaginable. This process of evolution is ongoing. The more we are inspired to broaden our knowledge and perspectives on how things work in our lives, the more we have the potential to achieve.

Today's objective is to zero in on a certain task or responsibility. create opportunities where there were none before. Create a list of all the possible ways that your wildest dreams could become a reality one day.

Sunday, February 28

> To fix one's attention on the physical self is to invite death, whereas to center one's thoughts on the Holy Spirit is to invite life and peace.

Due to the fact that I have battled an eating disorder for a significant portion of my life, I have spent much too much time concentrating on the outside rather than the inside of my body. In some respects, I was already dead inside. When I started focusing on myself and on who I actually was, I was able to start developing a loving connection with myself. [Case in point:] Not until then did I experience the feeling of being truly safe and attractive in my own skin.

Your objective should be to focus on the qualities that you possess on the inside that contribute to your attractiveness to others. Make a list of five to ten of the nonphysical aspects of your personality that contribute to the fact that you are an exceptional human being.

Month March, Chapter 3

March 1

> The perfect present for someone who has everything Sometimes the most valuable thing you can give another person is yourself.

When I was thirteen years old, I gave the church that I attended $150 that I had earned from babysitting. Because I was so proud of myself for carrying out this kind deed, I felt compelled to inform everyone that I knew about it. Later in that day, I couldn't place my finger on why, but I began to have second thoughts about how thoughtful I had been. I was aware that I was not solely motivated by altruism but also by the possibility of receiving praise for my efforts. It is of the utmost importance to perform acts of kindness for other people without expecting anything in return. A single act of kindness can mean a lot and help both the person who receives it and the person who does it in ways that are hard to fully understand.

The objective is to secretly carry out a kind deed of compassion for another person. Today, show some consideration to a person you don't know by doing something nice for them, and don't ask for anything in return, so you can experience the joy of giving.

March 2

> Hatred is just an extreme form of love that can't talk about how it feels in a logical or reasonable way.

At school, I was fuming because of the bullies I had to deal with. I came to see that harboring resentment toward other individuals just served to make me feel worse about myself. I ended up shifting my anxieties away from myself and onto other people. From there, a domino effect begins. If I had been more resolute and confident in my capacity to love myself, I would have been in a better position to find more productive ways to deal with the negativity that surrounded me and to rise above it.

You must not give into your hatred, or it will control you. Today, have compassion for your bullies by realizing that their actions are caused by the pain and suffering they are going through themselves.

March 3

> The question is not who will let me, but rather who will prevent me from doing it.

If I had believed everyone who told me I didn't have what it takes, I wouldn't be anywhere near where I am now. Developing self-assurance was a process that required some time on my part. It could seem terrifying, but it's best to confront the challenge and overcome your worries because, in the end, those other people won't make a difference.

I stopped giving any thought to all of the nonsense that occurred along the way. Instead of worrying about not succeeding, I gave up trying to control my future and instead let the things that I enjoy doing the most take the driver's seat. The only person who could have prevented me from continuing was myself. When I run into people who tell me I can't accomplish anything, it only serves as a reminder that I shouldn't pay attention to what they have to say. But the only person I believe in is myself.

Is there someone in your life who makes it a habit of undermining your efforts to achieve success? It's time to either have a conversation with them or cut them out of your life completely.

March 4

> When two people are able to hear each other out and get an understanding of where the other person is coming from, a bond of trust is created between them. From what I've seen, this is the thing that makes friendships and romantic relationships work.

Relationships with members of one's own family, with friends and acquaintances, with significant others, and with those with whom one works are not only complicated but also rich in educational opportunities. Nobody is born knowing everything there is to know about the world. Everyone goes through a variety of situations, has failures, achieves success, and then goes on to make other mistakes from which they can learn. The ability to trust and pay attention to the people you share your life with is the cornerstone of all healthy relationships.

Aim: When you are having a conversation with friends, you should make sure that you are paying attention to what they are saying and that you are not preoccupied with anything else. You are responsible for that, and you anticipate receiving the same treatment in return.

March 5

> We now live in a world in which humans have set foot on the moon. This momentous occasion occurred on March 5. It is not a miracle; we simply made the decision to travel.

The vast majority of our wildest dreams can become a reality. When we look up at the sky and see the moon so far away, the idea that a person may have ever been on the moon seems impossible and unintelligible to us. But it was humanity that made everything happen, and at the beginning, it all started with a wish.

The mission for the day is to have faith in the unthinkable. After all, there's always a chance it won't be impossible.

March 6

> I am grateful for all of the love and heartbreak that I have experienced during the course of my life. Each has its merits.

When it comes to love, I've experienced everything from happiness to heartbreak and every emotion in between as a black woman. As I've grown older, I've realized that the challenging aspects of life are simply a natural part of living and that they help make me stronger. As a result, I've acquired the ability to accept these aspects of life. It is painful to persevere through the challenging times, but much like a muscle, this area of your life needs to be worked out in order to become stronger.

The goal of this exercise is to reflect on a difficult time in your life and then think about how, contrary to your expectations, the awful feeling did not last forever. Keep in mind that life continues on and that only time can truly heal the wounds that have been suffered.

March 7

> The only way to have a friend is to be a friend to others.

You can't expect other people to treat you well if you don't treat the other people you interact with well first. When you need a friend, you often don't know how to be a good friend to others. As youngsters, we were all taught the "golden rule," which states that we should treat others in the same manner that we would like to be treated ourselves. Although it may sound trite, if more individuals adhered to this ethic, the world would be a far better place.

The goal is to think of something you would appreciate if one of your friends did something nice for you and then do that favor for that person. Consider the ways in which you interact with other people.

March 8

> Every one of our actions has some kind of consequence. What we put out into the world will one day come back to haunt us; therefore, we should always act lovingly toward one another.

It is critical that our behaviors and the manner in which we interact with others be marked by attentiveness and consideration. You can't tiptoe around other people like you're walking on eggshells, but you still need to treat them with genuine care and respect. When you act spitefully or enviously toward another person, you need to be ready to deal with the consequences of your actions.

Today's mission is to bring a smile to the face of at least fifteen different people. The race with a friend to see who can get to fifteen points first is a lot of fun and should be done whenever possible. There's no telling when those people will give you a reason to smile again, just when you need it the most.

March 9

> I don't need to sing if I'm going to sing like someone else.

You have to go through life being the real you. It is imperative that you have a sufficient understanding of who you are in order to be faithful to yourself when someone else wants you to be someone else. The most attractive characteristics are self-assurance and an absence of concern for what other people think of you. After all, the majority of people are able to see right through you when you try to pass yourself off as someone else.

The objective is to perform your own music and dance in your own unique way. You are not obligated to imitate or behave in the same manner as anyone else.

March 10

> There is a crack in everything, and that is how light may penetrate it.

My life has been filled with so much beauty and pleasure thanks to the difficult experiences I've had to go through. When I finally make it out of the shadows, I will be able to appreciate the fact that it is over. The torment forced me to mature and become someone who is better, stronger, and more grateful for everything that life has to offer as a result of the shift. It may appear that there is a long distance between you and the light at the end of the tunnel, but the more faith you have, the sooner you will see it.

The objective is to discover reasons for hope despite the dire circumstances.

March 11

> It is important to not be scared to stand up for what you believe in, even if it means doing so by yourself.

There will be times in your life when you feel as though you are the only person who sees things from your point of view. It truly doesn't matter what other people think as long as you always follow your heart and conscience and respect what seems right to you. If you do that, then it won't matter what other people say. You have to keep your job and act in a morally responsible manner. Throughout the course of history, efforts for civil rights have traditionally started with a small group of individuals. They were ridiculed by everyone, yet they did not back down from their position. Last but not least, those movements changed the course of history by blazing a trail that allowed so many outstanding people to be accorded respect and equality in later years.

The mission for the day is to speak up for a cause or an individual. It could be a total stranger, but it could also be someone you care about.

You might also consider joining forces with a group of people who are already fighting for the same cause as you.

The 12th of March

> If you honor every sensation, you will be able to live a genuine life.

One of the aspects of life that I've come to enjoy more and more is the fact that it is never just made up of one thing. At various points in our lives, we experience feelings of delight, boredom, loss, and grief. All of these feelings intertwine with one another to create the structure of our lives. We aren't able to influence everything that happens to us, but we can control how we react to the many situations we find ourselves in. I used to view every obstacle as a huge roadblock and a personal reflection on the trajectory of my goals and dreams for the future. Now I realize that as long as I respect myself authentically in every moment and as long as I know that life will be filled with every hue of emotion, every texture of sensation, and that there is beauty in it, life will be filled with every shade of emotion, every texture of sensation, and that there is beauty in it.

Goal: Think about someone or something that broke your heart, and then think about how that experience helped you develop and grow in positive ways as a result of it. God, please grant me the serenity to accept the things that I cannot change, the courage to change the things that I can change, and the discernment to know the difference. On

March 13th.

> O Lord Jesus Christ, give me the peace to accept the things I cannot change, the courage to change the things I can, and the discernment to know the difference.

I would want to say the serenity prayer because today is the first anniversary of my decision to abstain from using drugs or alcohol. It is common practice for people in recovery to recite this prayer on a regular basis; nevertheless, the fact that one does not need to be in recovery in order to recite these lines is among the many wonderful things about this prayer.

Because of this prayer, which I have essentially recited on a daily basis during my healing process, I have been able to reduce the tumult of complex feelings and thoughts that frequently wash over me, particularly on days when I am feeling particularly down. In life, we all try our hardest and try to take things one day at a time; yet, there are times when we just need a simple reminder of the fact that we do our best.

Aim: Recite this prayer aloud today, either to yourself or to a friend, and notice how it makes you feel. You should try to do that every day for a week and allow it to change your perspective.

March 14

> Find the light that shines from within you, and then share it with the world.

Everyone has their own special gift that they can give to the world and share with others. Every one of us is simply wandering around aimlessly, trying to figure out our lives, and we all go about it in our own special way. That particular kind of self-discovery captivates my interest. You have a light within you, and in order to see things more clearly, we require that light from you. Because our vision would be severely impaired without it, you must not let anyone turn down the light.

The objective is to let your light shine. What are some ways that you can help others see the light?

15 March

> What are you attempting to escape if you spend your entire life looking for the next party to attend?

There are a lot of celebrities in popular music and culture who want people to believe that they are tough and powerful because they party all night and use drugs. My understanding of what it means to be strong is that you are able to bear your difficulties and acknowledge your emotions without feeling the need to hide them. On some nights, I've had to fight the urge to act out, either because I'm physically unable to stay still in the pain or because I'm trying to avoid living in the moment by doing something else.

Your mission is to put an end to your running and get on with dealing with your problems and your life. It may be as simple as refraining from checking your phone while you are by yourself or in an awkward situation. Pay attention to what is going on in your head and value the ideas that come to you. Pay attention to what is going on in your head.

March 16

> It's either win big or go home. As far as we know, this is the last time any of us will ever be in this place; therefore, we should let go of our worries and concentrate on achieving our goals.

Don't let another second of your life pass without engaging in activities that bring you joy. Your dreams belong to you for a reason; consequently, you should go after them with both hands wide open. Because I was clear about what I wanted out of life and worked extremely hard to get it, I've been able to achieve a lot in my time here on earth.

Big goals used to scare me, but as I started achieving them, I started to embrace them, and they started to embrace me in return. Now, I can't imagine my life without them.

Your mission is to document every aspiration you have for your life. Always keep in mind that there is no dream that is out of your reach. You have the power to take over the entire globe.

Do Not Make Any Assumptions on March 17th.

> Find the courage to ask questions and express what it is that you really want.

Keep your communication with other people as straightforward as you possibly can to avoid misunderstandings, misery, and drama. You only need to make one agreement to bring about a significant shift in your life.

It is better to take the time to ask questions and find the words to describe how you truly feel than to rush through the process. When we are in a rush or reluctant to tell the whole truth, we frequently leave a lot of room for interpretation. Unfortunately, this is the point at which miscommunications start to take place. Ask a person what they are thinking or how they are feeling if you are unsure of what they are saying or how they are feeling.

March 18

> Instead of making assumptions about what the truth is, muster the courage to find out.

It would be beneficial for you to have a clear head, and you would be aware of the specific action that someone takes as well as his objectives.

March 19

In each and every community, there is perpetually more work that has to be done. Every nation has wounds that need to be treated and healed. Each and every heart possesses the potential to do so.

It is essential that you do not permit such melancholy to overtake you and cause you to become so despondent that you drown in it. Considering all of the problems, disasters, and tragedies that we hear about on a daily basis, the presence of darkness does not preclude the presence of light. Storms can sometimes produce the most amazing rainbows after they have passed through an area.

Your mission for today is to consider what you may do to spread love, hope, and faith to others around you. Think about whether there is somebody in your life who could benefit from your help.

March 20

You can't repair other people's issues, but you can sit with them and share their burden, which will make those troubles easier to bear.

When we are trying to comfort loved ones, all we want to do is take away the suffering that they are experiencing. When we care about someone, it is natural for us to want to assist them when they are in need. Having said that, there are a lot of circumstances in which people have to go through misery in order to properly learn and come out of it stronger than they were before. Keep in mind that you should not help someone who is currently in need of assistance. Help them come up with a solution to the problem.

The next time a loved one you care about is going through a challenging time, your mission is to think about how you can help them rather than how you can fix them.

21st of March

> One should never pass judgment on a book based solely on its cover.

It is far too simple to pass someone on the street and form snap judgments about who they are based on a passing detail or flaw in their appearance. It's possible that they have an unfriendly manner about them. It's possible that they aren't as outgoing as you are. In any event, you have no right to judge another person unless you have taken the time to get to know them and learn about the things that have happened in their lives. The things that we observe on the surface are simply that: impressions that are only on the surface, and they do not teach you anything about what other people have actually gone through in their lives.

Spend some time getting to know someone by talking to them about themselves and actively listening to what they have to say. This is the goal.

March 22

> My perspective is that life is a blessing, but simply existing does not mean that a person is alive.

Life is precious, and the things you accomplish with it are what determine whether or not you feel truly alive on the inside. It is not sufficient to merely exist and take that gift for granted; one must go beyond this. Fear is something that affects each and every one of us, but the more we work to overcome our worries, the more we may take pleasure in life. One's perspective and prior experiences can significantly shape their feelings of fear. When I was thirteen years old, I was a passenger in a car that was involved in a catastrophic accident. Even to this day, the prospect of getting into a vehicle causes me a wide variety of different worries. But the fact of the matter is that if you spend your whole life in terror, you aren't really living at all.

The challenge for today is to face one of your fears head-on.

The 23rd of March

> The ability to evaluate a thought without accepting it as one's own is a sign of a mind that has been properly trained.

There is a great deal of ignorance in the world today. Conflict, bloodshed, hatred, condemnation, intolerance, and sorrow are all products of ignorance. Ignorance begets. If we try, regardless of our level of education, each of us has the opportunity and capability to seek out new information and acquire comprehension of the subject at hand. Even if your ideals are different from those of other people or if you disagree with them, each of us ought to be more receptive to criticism and to the perspectives of others.

Listen to different points of view, and then form your own opinions based on what you've heard. If you disagree with someone, it's best to agree to disagree in a civil way.

March 24

> Regardless of how much my heart may hurt, I will never stop being grateful that it is still able to beat.

In my twenty-one years, I've been through a lot of painful breakups in romantic relationships. Relationships may be fun, exciting, beautiful, and alluring all at the same time. However, in addition to that, it is difficult. I am aware that we will all, at some point in our lives, be confronted by terrible events, but now that they have occurred, I am going to let myself feel the sorrow. Despite the fact that it hurts, I am reminded that it was worthwhile since I was able to feel things to such a great degree of depth. The very fact that I was able to experience such love and let someone into my heart is evidence that I am still alive and that I am capable of a great deal.

The objective is to feel an overwhelming sense of gratitude toward everyone who has entered your life, whether for good or for ill, because they have all served to educate you in some way.

March 25

> Keep in mind that there is a little girl hiding inside of you, and speak to her as if you have just met her today.

It never ceases to amaze me how readily we are able to look down on ourselves and our accomplishments. We don't realize how much damage we're doing to ourselves when we fall into the habit of saying nasty things about ourselves, but we do it anyway. Would you tell your younger self these things when you were four years old? Instead of taking care of myself when I'm sick or exhausted at work, I push through it and continue to work as though nothing is wrong. I tend to forget that I still harbor a vulnerable little child inside of me. Always ask that of oneself before criticizing oneself, and then refrain from doing so. What steps would you take in the event that a child fell ill? It is imperative that one always prioritizes their own health and well-being.

Be gentle with yourself; that is the goal. Give your inner child as much love and attention as you would your own child.

March 26

> Why bother trying to fit in when you were designed to stick out from the crowd?

Recognize and embrace all of your peculiarities. We are not created to fit in; we are all unique. There are instances when we mistakenly assume that we have to hide our differences, but this is not the case. Trying to figure out who you are and what your life's purpose is can be a nerve-wracking experience for some people. But getting the answer is really important if you want to accept yourself and be true to yourself.

Don't try to hide who you are from yourself; instead, present that version of yourself to the world and be proud of it.

March 27

I know there will never be a day when I don't stress about what I eat or how my body looks, but I'm learning to live with it, and I wish I could share with younger women the importance of locating and maintaining a comfort zone.

In a culture that places such a high premium on outward appearances, feelings of insecurity are natural and common for everyone, regardless of gender. People go through hardships on a daily basis, but we still find it within ourselves to persevere and keep our strength. We are not defined by the things that we put into our bodies, and neither are the mistakes that we make.

As a goal, you should strive to transcend the shallow body-image ideals of society. You are superior to that, and you have earned the right to be who you are.

28 March

What you fight against will last.

If you spend an excessive amount of time dreading something rather than letting go of it, you are drawing the energy and concepts associated with that thing into your life.

The goal is to have faith that you will be provided for in this life and to refrain from concentrating on or worrying about the other things.

March 29

> Pay attention to the stories told by other individuals and search for the grace and bravery that others have displayed in their actions.

Hearing the stories of those who admire me is inspiring, which is why I enjoy listening to them. It's astonishing how much power we all have within us because they tell me about how they overcame things like bullying, eating disorders, addictions, and self-harming behaviors like cutting. I also believe that sharing your experiences with others will help you become stronger and will magnify the positive influence that you have on the lives of others. Being vulnerable and opening up to other people takes courage.

Objective: Give a friend who is struggling a call and describe a time in your life when you had to overcome a challenge and how you did it.

March 30

> Taking the path of least resistance will invariably be appealing and pursued.

Our principles will be scrutinized thoroughly at all times. There will always be the temptation to take the path of least resistance—to lie, cheat, and steal—since these actions appear to be less difficult in the present, but I guarantee that these choices will come back to haunt you in the end. I can't stress enough how important it is to give yourself a reality check before acting in a way that you'll later regret. Don't give in to peer pressure or let other people's actions or decisions change you in any way.

Objective: If you have a friend or coworker who lies, cheats, or steals, it is imperative that you let them know that their values do not match yours, particularly when their poor behaviors begin to affect you. This is especially important when their negative behaviors begin to influence you at work.

March 31

The presence of doubt is really annoying. However, he is too lonely to recognize that Faith is actually his twin brother.

You are not a fool; therefore, stop treating yourself as if you are on April 1st, because that is April Fools' Day. Put your faith in yourself and your discerning abilities, and listen to your gut instincts. We are all endowed with the capacity for intuitive thought.

Aim: Whenever you catch yourself doubting who you are or what you're capable of, you should immediately stop and tell yourself, "I believe in myself."

Month April, Chapter 4

April 1

Sometimes, someone can really surprise you. not in terms of the way they seem. not in accordance with the assertions that they make. They are completely unchangeable in their nature.

It is far too simple to allow oneself to become entranced by the world's superficial splendor. It is astonishing how you might meet someone who has a beautiful appearance but later discover that they are lacking in basic manners and consideration for the feelings of others. The moment a person exhibits harsh behavior toward other people, all potential for physical attractiveness that they might have evaporates. The origins of genuine beauty can be found in virtues such as kindness and compassion. A cursory inspection is not enough to fully appreciate such stunning beauty.

Your goal is to spend time getting to know people and then evaluating how beautiful they are; as a result, you will become more attractive to other people.

April 2

Remember that deeds speak louder than words.

I am constantly working to become a better person by analyzing the impact that my day-to-day actions have on other people. I always make it a point to apologize to the person I've wronged as soon as I realize that my actions have caused them harm. It is an awesome feeling when I make a conscious effort to recognize my shortcomings and then do everything in my power to repair them and demonstrate love for myself. These actions have considerably more weight than the words that are said.

Objective: Think about who you ought to get in touch with, whether it be to say sorry or to get back in touch with them, to tell them you love them or to convey your regrets.

April 3

> The race is best appreciated when run at a slow and steady pace.

Although we've all heard the expression "slow and steady wins the race," I find that even though I agree with it, I enjoy the idea of taking it easy so that I can appreciate the little things in life even more. In today's fast-paced environment, it is easy to get into a habit of hurried behavior, and there are moments when we don't even have time to catch our breath. This is not only harmful to our bodies and the amount of stress we are experiencing, but it also makes whatever we are doing far less enjoyable.

I've recently come to the realization that time moves really quickly, and if I don't stop and try to slow down, I end up missing the smaller moments in life. So, no matter where you're going or what you're trying to achieve, it's important to enjoy the journey itself. Otherwise, what's the point?

Take 10 slow, deep breaths and then attempt to meditate or do something calming whenever you feel yourself beginning to become overwhelmed by the demands of your busy life.

April 4

> No one has ever tried to figure out how much information the human heart can hold, not even poets.

It is truly incredible how much love the heart can hold, and there is no doubt in my mind that love is worth the anguish and agony that it inevitably brings with it. Think about all of the lovely things that come along with love, particularly in the beginning: the butterflies in your stomach and the giddiness that you feel all over your body. The way that love makes me feel is unlike anything else in the entire world, and I wouldn't trade it for anything.

The goal is to get rid of anything that stops you from letting out all of your feelings without being afraid that they will hurt you.

April 5

> Every single one of us is a work in progress.

Nobody has ever told you that you needed to have everything sorted out, and I can promise you that nobody else does either. The most important thing is that you continue to work on yourself, that you give yourself permission to heal, grow, and learn, and that you keep your humility. When you reach the point where you believe you have completed your assignment, start over and remind yourself that the effort was well worth it.

The objective is to recognize that you are a work in progress. Think back on the past year and assess how much you've grown and developed in that time. Think about the ways in which you will develop throughout the course of your entire life, year after year. Which of the many aspects of yourself do you feel could use some work right now?

April 6

> Recovery is something that you have to work on every single day, and it does not take a day off. You cannot afford to take a day off from it.

Maintaining sobriety is not always an easy task. I have days that are good and days that are horrible, but the bad days are the days when I know I need to get help, which is not an easy thing to do. We are all dealing with something, whether it be a physical addiction, a mental health issue, a handicap, or an emotional trauma. We all have something that we are going through. The aim is not to achieve perfection in this endeavor. It's as simple as becoming the physically and mentally healthiest version of yourself that you can be.

Goal: What kinds of traumatic experiences are you working through? What kinds of challenges are you now facing? You can help yourself by reaching out to a friend or seeking support from a professional.

April 7

In my opinion, the benefits of time spent by oneself cannot be overstated. You have to get used to being alone without relying on the company of others to define who you are.

Being alone does not necessarily make things simple. Not only has it become easier for me to spend more quality time by myself, but I've also started to value my solitude in the process of doing so. It is essential to be able to find peace and enjoyment in your time spent by yourself, regardless of whether you are an introvert or an extrovert. When we spend time alone, we may truly get to know who we are, which in turn makes us stronger people, better friends, and eventually, better people.

The objective is to find comfort in quiet time spent with one's own thoughts.

April 8

The most heartbreaking aspects of being impoverished are feelings of isolation and worthlessness.

It is irrelevant how much cash you have in your possession. A person's affection or goodwill cannot be purchased with monetary compensation. Everyone has the basic human need to feel loved and cared for, and this yearning has nothing to do with material success. The love and the people who are in your life are more essential than any amount of money that could ever be earned.

The mission for the day is to go above and beyond in order to make someone else feel treasured and loved.

April 9

> Put your energy into developing a successful relationship. Establish your goals, and don't forget to dream.

It's great to have lofty goals, but in order to realize those dreams, you need to break them down into more manageable chunks and put them in writing. Simply taking them into consideration is not enough; you must go out and look for them. After putting in a lot of effort to make a dream come true, one of the most satisfying experiences is crossing an accomplished objective off of one's list.

Create a list of everything you want to accomplish in the coming year. Keep your concentration and start crossing things off your list as soon as you can.

The 10th of April:

> Become the beneficial change that you wish to see in the world.

When you show others how to create the world they should be living in through your actions, they will be more likely to follow your lead. It really is as simple as that. If you want things to change, you have to be the one to bring about that change.

Create a list of the things that are important to you, and don't be afraid to stand up for the things that are important to you.

April 11

> Just like everyone else, I am a collection of flaws that were pieced together with the best of intentions.

Every single one of us is flawed and broken in our own unique ways. We never had any intention of going out into the world and becoming flawed, but that's how things operate in life; we make mistakes and we learn from them. That is what separates us from everyone else.

The goal is to be nicer and more kind to oneself. Learn to be grateful for the lessons that your flaws have taught you and accept them as part of who you are.

April 12

> What a wonderful thing it is that nobody needs to wait even one second before getting started on making the world a better place.

Recently, I happened to be walking by a homeless man and watched as other people walked past him as well. Because that made me feel so miserable, I had to stop what I was doing and have a conversation with him. Following my introduction of myself, he then went on to introduce himself as Denny. As he told me some jokes, we started having a conversation and laughing it up together.

After a while, he started crying and thanking me for what I had done. When I asked him why, he explained that it was the first time in several days that anybody had talked to him. He couldn't hide his happiness or his appreciation at having the chance to talk to another person, so he did both. I couldn't fathom how something as straightforward as that could give us both so much pleasure. That is a moment in time that I will never, ever forget.

The mission for today is to make someone else's day better by doing something nice for them.

13 April

> There is no reason to worry about tomorrow when we have been given the opportunity to enjoy today.

I understand that everyone is worried about what may happen next, but based on my previous experiences, I've found that this line of thinking is counterproductive. It does nothing but make you feel more stressed out, and the majority of the time, your mind is preoccupied with things that may or may not come to pass. We only have today and this moment in time, so all we can do is focus on being here and now, count our blessings for today, and have faith that everything else will work out.

Your task for the day is to reflect on all of the things for which you are grateful.

April 14

Proceed with caution. Your future self will thank you for it.

Every decision you make right now will have some bearing on the rest of your life. All of these things, including the foods you tell yourself, the substances you put in your body, and the people you surround yourself with, are going to stay with you. Regardless of whether it's been ten days or ten years, it's critical to be mindful of how you treat yourself at all times. Keeping this in mind, it is essential to think about the situation in a broader context.

Your mission is to counteract every damaging thought you have about yourself by replacing it with its polar opposite. Think about how quickly you could modify your behavior if you were more conscious and more positive.

April 15

I place a higher priority on how I feel about myself than I do on how I appear to others. True beauty comes from being able to be yourself while still feeling at peace and happy.

You were born with your body and your looks, so be grateful for what you have been given and don't let anyone else take credit for it. Spencer West has spent his entire life without legs, but this has not stopped him from living life to the fullest and making the most of every opportunity. When I start to be critical of my body, I think about Spencer's incredible strength, and I realize how fortunate I am to have legs at all. I am fortunate to have legs. If he can do it without legs, then I can do it too.

The objective here is to appreciate what you have by imagining what it would be like to be in the shoes of another person.

April 16

> Now or never is the only option.

Only the present remains. This is something I've realized after going to a large number of events and performances, the majority of which I can hardly recall. It was due to the fact that I wasn't living in the moment at the time. I was performing the task at hand without paying attention to it.

Put an end to all distractions, step away from your phone or computer, and just focus on enjoying the present moment.

April 17

> You are only as powerful as the member of your team who is the weakest, and you are only as hopeful as the partner who brings you the most down.

You are the sum of your friends, so it is important to be aware of who you are associating with and what their values are. It is essential that we are aware of the significant impact that our friends have on both ourselves and vice versa. It's possible that this will turn out to be a beautiful experience if your friends are full of love, devotion, respect, and optimism for you.

Is there someone in your life who constantly brings you down and makes you feel terrible about who you are? If there is, this might be a good time to have a conversation with the relevant person in order to work out how to address the issue in question.

April 18

> When one door closes, another one opens. However, we often focus so much on the door that has closed and feel so sad about it that we miss the door that has opened for us.

In spite of everything that you are going through, there is always going to be a way out of this situation. Although getting there might appear to be an uphill battle, it is not impossible. You'll start to see the positive side of things if you just keep plugging away at it. It has come to my attention that there is always something to anticipate with excitement. It doesn't matter how great or small the difficulties are; it helps me get over them.

Goal: Keep in mind that this horrible time will eventually be behind you and that better times are just around the corner.

April 19

> I hope that you get the chance to live as long as you want and as long as you don't want to live.

Our lives are composed of the beautiful things that we choose to surround ourselves with; the more splendor that we choose to immerse ourselves in, the more complete our lives will be. However, the pursuit of ever-greater quantities stops us from appreciating what we already have. In this life, it is only natural to want things, but it is also vital to refrain from being greedy.

Appreciate what you already have rather than fixating on what you don't have and working hard to get more. This is the goal.

April 20

Try to focus on how far you've already come rather than how much further you have to go. You are not where you want to be, but you are also not where you were before. This is progress.

The majority of our lives run at such a frenetic pace that we do not always have the opportunity to take a little break and consider how far we have progressed. In general, we have an unhealthy fixation on what will happen in the future. Nevertheless, it is essential to maintain the practice of checking in with oneself regularly.

We are continuously evolving. It's easy to feel dissatisfied with where you are in life if you don't take the time to recognize how far you've come and be grateful for it. It's not necessary to be exactly where you want to be, but the fact that you started is already a remarkable accomplishment. It is important to remember that anything worthwhile and any kind of advancement require time.

The goal for today is to take some time to reflect on how far you've come in the past year and to enjoy that success today. What are some things in your life that you have altered that you can look back on with pride?

April 21

Nobody is faultless. As long as we have the goal of becoming better, our shortcomings will continue to be a part of our journey.

How frequently do we engage in behaviors that we later label "bad" and subsequently feel remorse for our actions? As long as we take anything useful away from the experience, it was not for naught. We are not perfect, but rather than beating ourselves up about our shortcomings, we should look at them as opportunities to grow.

Your mission is to think about how you might use the things you regret as learning experiences for the future.

April 22

> There is no difference in the love that lies beneath it all.

Despite our individual quirks and skills, we are all made of the same flesh and blood. This unites us despite our differences. Both of our commonalities and our differences bind and link us together in equal measure. No matter how we choose to conduct our lives, we are all on a journey to discover how to know and love ourselves, as well as others, in a manner that is more profound and forthright.

Goal: Focus your attention on the things that unite you, your friends, your family, and the people you work with today.

April 23

> Permit yourself to see your life exactly the way you want it to look—bravely and fearlessly bringing your goals and dreams to fruition.

The use of our imaginations and the pictures we allow ourselves to conjure up are quite significant. It is essential for every one of us to have the mindset that we are capable of achieving our objectives, and I have no doubt in my mind that we will. To accomplish this, though, takes work; it is not something that just happens.

Therefore, rather than laughing it off because it is inconceivable, you should allow your imagination to run wild with all the things you want your life to be. Admit that you have a vision for your life and resolve to make achieving that vision a daily priority. There's a reason you keep thinking about it.

April 23

> Create a list of the accomplishments you want to achieve in the years to come.

It is essential that we pay attention to and show respect for the wisdom of our ancestors. We owe it to those who came before us to respect the wisdom and words of those who came before them.

When we travel through time, there are so many wonderful stories from our own family trees and history books that have the power to motivate and inspire us, but we tend to take them for granted. On the other hand, those people were the ones who paved the way for where we are now. It is essential that we not only take anything useful away from them but also keep in mind everything they have done for us and make sure to show our gratitude for it.

Learn something new today by cracking open a history book or researching a historical figure online that you are not familiar with. While you're doing it, do some research on one of your great-grandparents to find out more about who they were and what they stood for.

April 24

> Start from where you are now. Make the most of what you have. Give it your best shot.

No one anticipates that you will be perfect. It is sufficient to merely focus on doing the best you can right now with the resources at your disposal. A lot of the time, we put an excessive amount of pressure on ourselves to please other people.

Aim: It doesn't matter how you feel when you get up; all that matters are that you start where you are and make the most of today.

April 25

> I feel that the bulk of us admire powerful individuals. It is something we admire in others, desire for ourselves, and hope for our children, we want that for our children as well.

However, there are times when I wonder if we conflate the notion of power with words like hostility or even violence. In most people's views, strength is synonymous with aggressiveness. I believe that the students who tormented me, as well as bullies in general, are masking their actual feelings of grief by demeaning others, this includes the students who bullied me. It is probable that more individuals may be able to begin the healing process if they acknowledge their feelings and confess that they are vulnerable, unhappy, or helpless. Being so forthright and honest requires a giant degree of fortitude and courage.

Is it brave to act today, whether for yourself or for someone else?

April 26

> One of life's greatest pleasures is hearing a child guffaw and giggle themselves silly.

The uninhibited joy and exuberance with which a child laughs never fails to put a smile on my face. Children inhabit such a lovely and condensed version of the universe. They haven't seen, for the most part, a lot of the terrible things that are going on in the world around them, but adults have seen those things. The more we travel, the more we take in of the world around us. Both good and bad Therefore, when we see a child laughing at the silliest of things, it makes us long for a time in our lives when things were less complicated. It's healthy to look back on your adolescence with fondness, but you shouldn't allow those memories to rule your life. Take some time to appreciate where you are right now.

Laugh with a child today if the opportunity presents itself to you.

April 27

> One can get away from their problems by singing. This is an entirely new universe. No longer do I reside in this sphere.

Since I was a tiny kid, my voice has always been something that has helped me escape reality and find joy no matter where I am. Joy is something that everyone feels in their own way, and one of the most common ways to reach this state of happiness is to throw yourself into something.

Discover what brings you joy and allow yourself to soar above the skies while ensuring that both of your feet remain firmly planted on the ground. This is your goal.

April 28

> It's possible that stones and sticks could break her bones, but it's also possible that words and names could drive her insane.

People have the misconception that although rocks and stones can damage your bones, names can never hurt you. However, this couldn't be further from the truth. Names can be just as damaging as physical trauma. Words can sometimes inflict more emotional distress on us than actual physical pain. Words were spoken to me that came from my history and continue to cause me pain. I remember telling my mother that if the bullies had hit me or punched me instead of saying the horrible things they did, that would have been preferable since the things they said changed the course of my life forever.

The objective is to stand up for someone who is being bullied at their place of employment or education. Bring to mind, both for yourself and for others, the influence that words can have. And remember to be mindful of what you say when you are interacting with other people.

April 29

> A dreamer is required for the realization of any dream.

Always keep in mind that you are already equipped with the strength, patience, and drive to reach for the stars and make a difference in the world. We must all begin our journeys at some point, but it is important to keep in mind that our destinations are not fixed. Your hopes and ambitions will shift and develop alongside you as time passes. If you have an adventurous spirit and big dreams, the world is your oyster. Create a list of the top five to ten objectives that you want to accomplish in the upcoming month. Never give up on being the best possible version of yourself!

April 30

> You should gain wisdom from your errors and then impart that wisdom to others. Take pleasure in the here and now while keeping one eye on the future.

There is a significant difference between living in the past and gaining wisdom from its lessons. What's done is done, and I've learned that it's important to avoid dwelling on the past because I can't change what's already happened. On the other hand, I want to reflect on the past and take note of both my successes and failures so that I can improve in the future. However, at the end of the day, all we have is this moment, which we must cherish and adore, and the future is something that intrigues me as well.

Today, I encourage you to make a concerted effort to live in the here and now. Remind yourself that you are exactly where you need to be right now by bringing up the present whenever you find yourself concentrating on the past or being anxious about the future.

Month May, Chapter 5

May 1

> Instead of being judgmental, take an inquisitive approach.

It is essential that we maintain the sense of awe and curiosity that we possessed as children. When we are infants, we learn everything for the very first time, including how to crawl, eat, walk, talk, and experience sensations. As we get older, we tend to take for granted the things that are most fundamental. The more we keep an open mind and stay interested in the world around us, the more likely it is that we will find and learn new things.

Becoming an adventurer is the objective for the day. Nothing you see, hear, or feel should be taken as given at this point. Be open to taking a more in-depth look at things, and make it a point to educate yourself about the world around you.

May 2

> Take good care of yourself mentally, physically, and spiritually. You deserve it.

When it comes to criticizing ourselves, we are always the first to do so. When it comes to judging ourselves, we are our own harshest critics. And the process of learning to love who we are is an essential part of our journey. This involves taking care of all aspects of your being, including your mind, body, soul, and spirit. Observe how much of a difference it makes to your life if you treat yourself as you would a child. If you are kinder to yourself, you will see an improvement in everything.

The objective for today is to acknowledge who you are as a beautiful person by looking in the mirror.

May 3

> The day we decide not to say what we think about important things is the first day of the end of our lives.

It is essential to contribute because if you do not advocate for the causes in which you have faith, no one else will. What if you're supposed to help make a significant discovery on this planet, but you don't respect your own ideas enough to put them into action?

Aim: To have the confidence to speak out for what you believe in, to lead a meaningful life, and to be able to rest easy at night knowing that you are contributing in some way to making the world a better place. There is no better time than right now to enjoy what you have.

May 4

> Give them permission to read whatever they like, and then talk with them about what they've read.

If parents and children are able to have conversations together, there will be less need to restrict children's speech due to the decreased level of fear. It is essential for young people to have the sense that they are free to think and talk freely. Parents and teachers are expected to serve as positive examples for the children and students in their care. Their views and points of view shouldn't be disregarded in any way. Encourage children to recognize their value as well as their intelligence.

No matter how old you are, you should always make it a priority to inspire, care for, and encourage other people.

May 5

> No one is better than anyone else, regardless of whether they identify as gay, straight, lesbian, or bisexual.

Everyone is the same inside. If another person tries to persuade you otherwise, you have the choice to either engage in an open conversation with them or to leave the conversation altogether. You must not give in to the racism and hatred that they have.

Your goal should be to increase tolerance within your community.

May 6

> Never, ever settle.

People tend to be content with what they have because they are afraid that anything better will never come their way. They are concerned that they do not measure up to expectations. You are worthy of exactly what it is in life that you want, but you have to believe it; otherwise, you won't be able to attract it.

Aim: Give yourself a few moments to reflect on how valuable you are.

May 7

> Keeping resentment inside is like carrying a burning coal around with the intent of throwing it at someone else; you are the one who has been burned.

This is a lesson that I've had to learn numerous times in my life because it's so challenging to let go of things. Both anger and resentment are toxic emotions that can lead to self-inflicted wounds. Responding to wrongdoing with tolerance, forgiveness, and acceptance is the approach that should be used. In the end, it is best to let go of everything since otherwise, it would collect.

Your mission is to take a piece of paper, list everything that irritates you, and then burn the paper.

May 8

It is OK to act in a self-centered manner at times. It's possible that being fully selfless is bad for both your mind and your health.

They believe that if you are on an airplane that is going to crash, you should put your own oxygen mask on first before helping anyone else with theirs. You can't possibly look after others unless you first look after yourself. People make the mistake of mistaking it for selfishness, but in reality, it is the healthy kind of selfishness, the kind that enables you to devote your truest and most authentic self to the service of others.

The objective for today is to treat yourself to something nice, whether that be a massage, staying up late, or any form of meditation.

May 9

Determine a man's true value by looking at how he treats those below him in social standing rather than how he treats his peers.

When I observe someone being kind to a person in power while treating others harshly simply because they are lower on the social ladder in that person's opinion, there is nothing that turns me off more than that. I find it really repulsive. The manner in which a person treats different people can tell you a lot about who they are because it is the most transparent aspect of their character. If they don't, you might want to reevaluate your relationship with them.

Treat everyone the same way, with love, respect, and compassion, regardless of their income or social level. This should be your goal. You are not more or less deserving of respect than anyone else, regardless of the things you do or do not possess.

May 10

> Like the moon, emerge from your hiding place in the clouds! Shine.

Every single one of us will experience adversity at some point, but out of the gloom comes the dawn. You have the power and the ability to rise above whatever darkness or sadness is surrounding you, and you should make the effort to do so. Give permission for the light that resides within you to shine out into the world. It's possible that all it takes is thinking happy thoughts or smiling even when you don't feel like it to make a big difference.

Your goal should be to brighten everyone's day with a smile, even if you're experiencing feelings of depression.

May 11

> My mother always told me that if I became a soldier, I would eventually work my way up to the rank of general. If you live your life as a monk, you will one day become the Pope. Instead, I decided to become a painter like Picasso.

Without the love, companionship, and support of my great mother, I never would have made it to this point in my life. She never wavered in her support of me, even when I struggled to believe in myself. My confidence has grown because I know I can reach the goals I set for myself.

The importance of being honest, devoted, courageous, and loving is something that my mother instilled in me from a young age. I am very aware of the favor and blessing it is to have a mother of such high caliber.

Objective: Show appreciation to a loved one in your life for all the support and affection they've given you.

May 12

When we are preoccupied with what other people think of us, we give them the power to decide how we should spend our lives, and in the process, we lose touch with who we are without even realizing that we have done so.

We all have the need to be liked and loved, but when we put this desire ahead of loving ourselves first, we allow ourselves to become preoccupied with the opinions of others and stop living an authentic life. If someone insults you or calls you a name, you shouldn't let it get to you; instead, just keep quiet. Participating in the drama that they are creating will only do damage to your character.

The question at hand is: What makes you unique and sets you apart from others? Take one of your peculiarities and make it a daily part of your routine.

May 13

Don't put yourself through mental anguish by being envious. It is a foolish notion to feel that the life of another person is superior to your own when the reality is that we are all traveling down unique roads in life.

There are times in my life when I give in to the desire to be envious of another person's life, body, attire, or expertise. These are the times when I allow myself to be completely consumed by envy. It is a common experience to have this sense. It is commonly referred to as the "green-eyed monster" for a good reason. It is damaging to yourself, and while it is there, it consumes you completely. Maintain your strength, and don't fixate on the things that other people possess.

The goal here is to let go of any feelings of envy you may have for the life of another person and to give yourself permission to be truly glad that you are enjoying your own life.

May 14

> The only thing that is ever unpleasant about change is people's opposition to it. Change itself is never tough.

There is no way to steer clear of the fact that life is full of transitions. Recognize that your life will be full of transitions, and while this might be challenging at times, it is ultimately what forges our identities and motivates us to keep moving forward in life.

The goal is to accept the changes that are occurring in your life, regardless of how you feel about them. You are being propelled forward by all of these things, and beginning a new chapter in your life will include change. It is appropriate for you to feel thankful for all of your blessings.

May 15

> You hold the capacity to make significant changes in your life with nothing more than a shift of perspective.

My morning may not go as planned, and as a result, I may have feelings of depression or irritability. It's such a waste of the day that I'm even considering giving up on it. It is painful, and as a result, I may get impatient and lash out, which has repercussions for others. I recently learned that it is always possible for me to start a new day.

I just sit quietly and restart. I make the conscious decision to alter my mental attitude and remind myself that the day that lies ahead of me is packed with wonderful opportunities and advantages. In order to shift my mindset, I like to make a list of at least ten aspects of my life that I admire. When my mood changes, it affects the rest of my day in small ways.

The goal is to start keeping a daily record of gratitude. Every day, make a list of ten things for which you are grateful and keep it with you.

May 16

> Keep in mind that you need to take some deep breaths.

Even though it's an instinct that we're all born with, for some reason, it's the first thing that we forget, especially when we're under a lot of pressure and have a lot on our plates.

The objective is to concentrate on one's breathing while in a calm setting. It has the potential to significantly improve both your day and your mindset in a positive way.

May 17

> When someone I helped or in whom I had a great deal of faith acts unjustly toward me in some way despite the fact that he has behaved in terribly repulsive ways, may I still consider him to be my amazing teacher?

The ability to feel compassion for other people is essential to our pleasure. There is always the possibility that we will gain wisdom from people who have harmed us. It is difficult to go through life without experiencing some form of pain. Even our closest and most devoted friends might, on occasion, cause us to feel irritated. It is essential to keep in mind that even your closest friend is not an ideal companion for you. People in your immediate vicinity are also human. It is essential to acknowledge that they are prone to making mistakes.

Learn from everyone, including those who have hurt or failed you, for that is the goal here.

May 18

> You need to be brave and go forward in the direction of your goals. Enjoy yourself and make your dreams a reality.

If someone tells you that you can't live the life you desire, you don't have to prove them incorrect; instead, you should simply keep working hard and believe in your heart that you can live the life you want. Make use of the skepticism that they have shown you.

Your goal should be to pursue pleasure with every fiber of your being because you are deserving of all the joy in the world.

May 19

When it comes to our happiness, we can't always put our faith in the hands of other people. First, we need to look deep within ourselves to find it.

I've concluded that the most important thing is to strive to make yourself happy. You should never feel ashamed of how you are feeling because everyone goes through the same emotions at some point in their lives. Because, despite the fact that we may express them in different ways, they are fundamentally the same, we are able to connect with one another. You should never give someone the power to make you feel guilty about how you are currently feeling, since this is the single most crucial thing to keep in mind.

If you're having a bad day, you shouldn't expect other people to cheer you up or make you feel better.

May 20

Discover the joy that resides within you.

When we reach a certain point of maturity in life and start climbing our own personal ladders of success, we have to be careful not to let our egos get in the way of the integrity and honesty of the job that we do. Your ego will always be close behind you, following you and nibbling at your heels as you progress in this life. It will never be far away. Don't give in to the temptation to let it get to you.

Goal: Assess your ego's present position. Be aware of it and fight against giving in to its power.

May 21

> It's been proven that a simple grin can actually save lives.

Did you know that smiling can strengthen your immune system, which in turn can help you live a longer and happier life? Not only that, but because smiling is contagious, it can also make the people around you happier. When I was going through security at an airport, a TSA official suddenly smiled at me, and that one act completely changed the course of my day. When you make someone else happy, you also make your own day more enjoyable in the process.

The objective is to smile frequently since you never know whose day you may make better by doing so. One never knows how much of an impact a simple grin can have on the course of another person's life.

May 22

> When you throw dirt, you make yourself look worse.

Making the right choices is the name of the game in life. When someone shows disrespect toward us, we always have the option of replying to them. To respond with the same behavior that has angered us seems like it would be the most desirable thing in the world. Take into consideration the actual results it would produce.

When someone insults you in the future, your mission is to ask them in a kind and non-threatening manner how they would feel if you insulted them in the same way.

May 23

> True happiness comes from helping to motivate, encourage, and guide another person along a path that is good for that person in the long run.

There are many people in this world who are filled with envy. There can be moments when the wonderful news you share generates tension in a relationship. If you show them that you are supportive and happy for them, perhaps they will do the same for you.

In the future, when a close friend or member of your family shares some happy news with you, your mission will be to express true joy.

May 24

It is possible to bring about change by first listening to those whose actions you disagree with and then participating in debate with them.

In spite of the fact that there are over 7 billion people on earth, each of us is only equipped with a single brain as well as a unique collection of thoughts and principles. No matter how knowledgeable, empathetic, kind, open-minded, or enthusiastic we are, there will inevitably be times when we get something wrong. Even if we think that other people's ideas or belief systems are wrong, we cannot allow ourselves to become self-righteous about our own convictions and shut them out of consideration.

The goal is to keep an open mind and to accept that it's okay to be wrong sometimes. Investigate new areas of interest so that you can increase the scope of your perspective. You will benefit more from broadening your perspective and looking at things from a different angle if you can expand your mind.

May 25

I am a sluggish walker, but I never go backwards.

No matter what ails you, getting better is a process that takes time. No one can recover more quickly or more effectively than anyone else. It's not a race at all. You are required to move at your own pace, even if it is a snail's pace. There will be times when you want to give up; resist this urge. There will be times when you feel the need to slip, but you shouldn't. As long as you keep moving forward in your recovery at your own speed and avoid taking any steps backward, the only thing that matters is that you are making significant headway. Therefore, you should take pride in your successes for your own sake.

Your goal should be to avoid comparing the speed of your recovery to others'. Keep in mind that the rate at which each of us recovers physically, mentally, and emotionally is unique to that individual. Allow yourself the time you need and recognize that you deserve it.

May 26

> There is such a quick cycle of people entering and leaving your life. You should never miss a chance to show these people how much you appreciate them.

The experience of loss is an unavoidable component of existence. Throughout the years, a number of people who were very special to me have passed away. Despite the fact that nothing can ever bring them back, I am able to keep their spirit alive within me by thinking about them, their ideals, and the qualities that they possessed. This is an important sensation. The single most important thing to keep in mind is how we should prioritize spending the limited amount of time we have with the people who are important to us.

In memory of a loved one who is no longer with you, the goal for today is to pray or light a candle in their honor.

The date is May 27th.

> I am exactly where I should be at this moment in time.

I used to have no confidence in anything, including my higher power. I rejected everything. As a result of my recovery and ongoing efforts to adapt, I am finally able to acknowledge that I am exactly where I should be. My pleasure can be discovered alone at this very moment.

Your objective is to reflect on where you are in your life right now, including your achievements, relationships, and work, and to feel gratitude for the life you've created for yourself.

May 28

> The only thing that a parent can do for their child is to give them sound counsel or point them in the right direction, but the person themselves is ultimately responsible for how their character develops.

My parents, with all of their virtues and foibles, have played a significant role in shaping my journey thus far. Following my rehabilitation, I realized that I can gain wisdom from my parents and that it is ultimately up to me to shape my life into the kind of thing I envision it to be.

Your goal should be to show your parents how grateful you are for everything they have done for you and for giving you the gift of life.

May 29

> It is not thinking less of yourself that constitutes humility; rather, it is thinking less of yourself that constitutes humility.

There is a lot of hesitation among people when it comes to giving money to someone who is homeless. You can be of assistance by providing a person who is homeless with something nutritious to eat or drink by purchasing a meal or a bottle of water on their behalf. When I saw a homeless man, I suddenly remembered that I had some food in my purse that I could give to him. I addressed him with the following words: "I don't want to insult you, but if you're hungry, I'd love to offer this to you." He acted as if he had hit the proverbial jackpot. It was hard for me to comprehend how such a trivial thing could give him so much pleasure.

The goal for today is to go out of your way to help a person who is homeless or who needs assistance in some other way.

May 30

> There are always new possibilities available. The more resources that are put to use, the more will be available.

When I had finished composing my first few songs, I remember being concerned that I would never write any more songs. At the time, I was ignorant of the fact that the only way to continue to experience increased creativity was to keep producing.

The goal is to overcome any inhibitions that prevent you from expressing your creative side. There will be some that are remarkable, although there will also be some that are typical. Never give up trying.

May 31

> You were brought into this world for a certain reason.

There is a reason for each and every person and object that resides on this earth. There is no such thing as an identical twin. We are each wonderfully made and formed to carry out the tasks that have been assigned to us on this planet. Never let anyone convince you otherwise because you are priceless, exceptional, and lovely just the way you are.

The goal is to draw attention to the ways in which you stand out from other people and are special.

Month June, Chapter 6

June 1

> The act of thinking for oneself is perhaps the most courageous deed.

Every single one of us was endowed at birth with a special ability that is one of a kind and has the potential to revolutionize not just our own lives but also the wider world that is all around us.

I have lived my entire life seeing this, so I am certain that it is accurate. Whatever it is that you're really good at, there's a good chance that other people covet it. So, use your skills well, and you'll be surprised at how much you can inspire the people around you.

The mission for today is to motivate someone simply by being who you are.

June 2

> While no one is perfect, we may all strive to become better versions of ourselves.

Because life is a process, it incessantly provides us with new opportunities for growth and advancement. Every moment of every year is a chance to better oneself by being more confident, happier, and caring.

Make it your mission to improve yourself and motivate those in your immediate environment.

June 3

> Now is what constituting eternity.

Put an end to your search for the next big thing. You are currently engrossed in the process. As long as you continue to be in the here and now, the next moment will arrive exactly when it is supposed to. It is in our nature as humans to constantly be thinking about what we want out of life, where we are going next, and what we've already accomplished. Focus your attention on the here and now with the resources you currently possess.

The objective is to seize and keep in mind the present moment that you are in.

June 4

> You already have everything you could ever need within yourself.

Honesty is the path to discovering and connecting with one's true self. For me, the realization that I didn't have to go looking for answers anywhere else was a giant step toward recovery. Both the answers and the serenity were in my possession. When we do, it will be a considerable weight off our shoulders.

Today, I want you to look in the mirror and tell yourself, "I have everything I need right here, inside of me."

June 5

> The fact that we do not have enough resources is not our primary concern. Our greatest concern is that we possess an unlimited amount of power. It is not our darkness but rather our own illumination that causes us the most concern.

It is possible that you will experience fear at times when you realize what you are capable of achieving in this world. Everyone is born with the potential to accomplish amazing things in their life. They say that with great power comes tremendous duty; thus, accept and love your obligation to do something excellent with your life, as this saying goes, "with great power comes tremendous duty."

Aim: Make today count by accomplishing something meaningful with the assets at your disposal.

June 6

Rather than sobbing over the fact that it's over, you should be happy that it happened.

At some point, a wonderful experience or opportunity will come to an end. Focus your attention on the fact that it took place rather than ruminating on the fact that it is now over. After visiting Africa and spending time with my loved ones there, I found that I didn't want to return to the United States. When it was finally time for us to leave, we were all in tears because no one wanted to leave such a beautiful place. But now I am able to look back on it without crying. I have a lot of good memories from the time I got to spend there with the people that are important to me, and I can't wait to go again.

Your mission is to reflect on a happy period in your life and express gratitude for the joy that period offered you. Even though the good moments have passed, you should always remember them.

June 7

I'm torn between hope and despair at the moment.

Every person has to have access to a reliable support system. There have been times in my life when I've had to confront some challenging challenges; nevertheless, knowing that the people who follow me have faith in me and hope for my future helped me rediscover happiness. I was surprised to learn how much support I got from both my followers and the individuals in my immediate environment. To say how happy that makes me would be an understatement.

The purpose is to provide hope to someone who is going through difficult times. Let them know that you are accessible to speak with them at any time.

June 8

Love is not a sufficient guarantee of immaculate care. It is a form of active noun, very much like the word "struggle." To love somebody means to try to accept them just as they are at this moment.

One of the most challenging components of romantic relationships is coming to terms with the other person and accepting them for who they truly are. I can't tell you how many times I've wished I could change something about a friend or loved one, but then I remember that nobody, not even myself, is perfect. I can't tell you how many times I've wished I could change something about a friend or loved one.

Remember that no one, including yourself, is flawless, and keep that in mind whenever you find yourself condemning another person.

June 9

People are so unhappy in this world that they would choose to die rather than live as they are.

Bullies are responsible for the suicides of many young people today because they make their victims feel like they have no value. As someone who has been the target of bullying, I have personal experience with the dreadful and disturbing effects that can result from children making harsh comments. When a person is the target of cyberbullying, they may feel even more emboldened to hide behind their computers and say the most horrible things in their heads. It is the responsibility of each and every one of us to stand up for anyone who is being bullied or torn apart by mean-spirited words.

The goal for today is to advocate for someone else and make sure they realize how vital a role they play in the world.

June 10

> Do not idly wait for another people's approval while you sit around doing nothing. Any pleasure that comes from doing something you enjoy for yourself

If you don't love yourself first, it's impossible to truly love another person. If you are dissatisfied with who you are as a person, having a boyfriend or girlfriend will not change that fact, no matter how nice it is to be in a relationship. Only when you are awake, and only then, will you be able to see your significant other. It is always your consciousness rather than theirs that nods off to sleep on your pillow each night.

Whether you are currently in a relationship or not, your goal should be to spend some quality time connecting with yourself and getting to know yourself better.

June 11

> If you can only see yourself, you don't have a point of view since all you can see is yourself.

There are a lot of people walking around with inflated egos, convinced that they are better and more deserving than other people. No matter where we originate from or who we think we are, regardless of our beliefs, we are all human beings with beating hearts. People are quick to criticize one another and believe they are in the right, but you can't simply assume that your perspective is the correct one. You have to be willing to look beyond yourself. If you only care about the answers to your own questions, you're basically cutting yourself off from the rest of the world.

Aim: Before passing judgment on another person, try seeing yourself in their shoes and keeping in mind that they have the right to their own ideas and points of view. This will help you achieve your goal. They look at the world from a variety of different angles.

June 12

> Our destiny will not be predetermined by the stars, but by ourselves.

In life, we are constantly given numerous options from which to select. We are the creators of our opportunities, and for us to accomplish our goals, we need to have confidence in the skills that we possess. If we don't put ourselves through challenging situations, we'll never truly understand what it is that we're capable of doing.

The objective is to eliminate the practice of leaving significant decisions to chance. Take charge of the situation and make the decisions that will lead to the outcome you want.

June 13

> If I didn't love and accept myself, I wouldn't get very far in life.

It is not an easy task to cultivate the ability to love and accept oneself despite one's imperfections. During the course of my treatment and rehabilitation, I learned a great deal about myself. It instilled in me the importance of loving and accepting oneself first and foremost. I get new information on a daily basis. However, at the end of the day, I need to love myself first in order to be able to love anyone else. Learning how to successfully complete this task was challenging, but the rewards have been well worth the effort. Find the aspect of yourself that you dislike the most and train yourself to love it. This should be your goal.

June 14

> I am enormous and house a great number of people.

One of the reasons I was miserable for such a long time was because I never acknowledged my feelings; I was always trying to keep control. This was one of the reasons I was unhappy. When I didn't pay attention to how I was feeling, I was making the issue worse for myself. At first, I couldn't understand that this was the case. What I thought was keeping me sane was actually making me lose myself and feel like I had no control over my life. Once I started to accept my feelings, though, I started to feel like a whole person again.

The question is, what sensation have you been trying to avoid? Give yourself permission to pause, take a few deep breaths, and take in the experience. It is possible that it will feel worse at first, but if you let it in, you will find that it is not as frightening.

June 15

> You will find that you cannot hold on to things simply because they are burdensome.

Every day brings with-it brand-new opportunities for growth, and acknowledging that there are some situations over which we have no control is an essential component of that development. When we fixate on or worry about things that we can't change, we end up losing ourselves in the process. When we release something, we make space in our minds, our emotions, and our bodies for something more meaningful. When I finally let go of that spot in my heart, a flood of positive experiences and opportunities began to pour into my life.

Your goal should be to let go of anything or anyone that is harmful to you that you have been holding on to. You can either get rid of everything you've been holding on to or write a letter to the person you're having trouble letting go of.

June 16

Today is a day when we often look outside of ourselves for answers, satisfaction, and the chance to feel like we're whole.

I now see that when I was enthralled by my addictions, I was looking for solutions, happiness, tranquility, and love outside of myself. This is something I did not realize at the time. At the time, I had no notion that this was causing me a great deal of mental suffering. During my time in rehab, I learned how important it is to look inside yourself for answers and sources of strength.

Goal: Give more weight to what it is that you truly desire than to what other people anticipate you will do.

On June 17th,

Listen to what your gut is telling you to do.

There are several instances in our lives in which we struggle to make decisions, regardless of the significance of the options available to us. It's possible that our hearts are telling us one thing, our heads are telling us something else, and our friends are telling us yet another thing.

Before acting on what your heart truly believes to be the right course of action, it is essential to weigh all of the available options. Don't just follow what your close friends tell you to do; instead, make your own conclusions based on how you feel.

When you are faced with a decision in the future, your goal is to think about all of the options available to you, paying special attention to the options that come from your heart.

June 18

> Perform an act that people tell you cannot be done just once, and you will never again pay attention to the limitations they place on you.

One of the most liberating feelings in the world is when you prove to someone who doesn't believe in you what you're capable of achieving. When you experience this amazing feeling for the first time, you will understand that it is a complete waste of time to pay attention to those who try to convince you that there are limits to what you are capable of doing. It is in your best interest to use your time to show them and yourself that you are capable of achieving your goals. Always keep in mind that the only limit is the sky.

Your mission is to accomplish something that you have never been able to do in the past.

The nineteenth of June

> As long as we keep an open mind in the middle of pain, suffering, and hopelessness, there are many chances for growth and change.

You have an incredible opportunity to grow in both your faith and your strength whenever they are put to the test. Your interpretation of it is the only thing that matters. Although there are occasions when it may be challenging to ask for assistance, it is never a bad idea to do so. When things get difficult, I have vowed to myself that I will reach out for assistance and embrace that stage of my journey with open arms. This is a promise I have made to myself. I know that going through these problems will make me stronger and help my faith grow, but I won't be able to reach this goal if I don't keep an open mind about getting help from other people.

Aim: Maintain an open mind and look for help if you are going through a challenging time in your life. Because there are so many different resources available to help you out, you will never have to face a challenge by yourself.

June 20

> What you think, and not what you have or who you are, is the single most important factor in determining your level of happiness.

Genuine joy is something that everyone can experience, even if we have to work a little harder for it at times. If you've been feeling down, take a look at the kinds of ideas that have been going through your head. Perhaps you should even write them down so that you can see how your perspective on life has changed. If you become aware that the majority of your ideas are negative rather than positive, you need to make a serious effort to modify the way you are thinking.

First, jot down all of your negative ideas, and then, for each one, write down the positive thinking that counters it. While you do this, stand in front of the mirror and recite the positive affirmations to yourself.

June 21

> You've come for a purpose. Put your skills and talents to good use.

Put your skills to use to help make the world a better place, no matter what those skills may be. Because no one else possesses what you do, you must put your knowledge and experience to use in order to contribute to the betterment of the world. If you don't believe in yourself and don't try to make the world a better place, you'll never know how much of an impact you are capable of having on the globe.

Select the problems that are most important to you and determine how you can best help or benefit them. This is your goal.

June 22

> The suffering will eventually end, but the beauty will remain.

It is impossible to understand anything other than the immense grief that we are experiencing when we are going through trying times and horrible circumstances. This is because the two go hand in hand.

Despite this, there is always a ray of hope at the end of the tunnel. I've realized that although sadness eventually passes away, the beauty that emerges as a result of your growth will remain forever. One day, you'll be able to reflect on your past experiences and value the things you've learned.

The objective is to avoid getting caught up in the discomfort since it will pass.

June 23

> Far too many of us are choosing to live our lives based on our anxieties rather than our ambitions.

You are unable to take any action because of your fear. Fear should not be allowed to prevent you from achieving your goals, particularly your ambitions. You might already know this, but FEAR is an acronym that stands for "False Evidence Appearing Real."

In other words, your worries aren't real since they're based on things that haven't happened yet and, as a result, don't exist. As a result, you shouldn't be concerned about them.

Instead of focusing on a fear, you should focus on a goal or a hope for your life. This will help you reach your life's goal.

June 24

> **What we think about manifests in our lives.**

Because the thoughts we have are so strong, we need to make sure that we are always conscious of what it is that we are telling ourselves. Whatever it is that we have in mind has the potential to become a reality thanks to the power of our ideas. So frequently, we may get into a pattern of pessimistic thinking without even being aware that we are doing so, and before we even realize it, we may have brought into our lives the very thing that we feared it would bring.

The encouraging news is that one may apply this concept to one's optimistic ideas as well. When we have optimistic thoughts about our lives, the energy of our perspective has the power to change those lives without our conscious awareness.

Aim: Devote today to contemplating the factors that will contribute to your success in achieving your goals. Get rid of the bad thoughts that are plaguing your head.

June 25

> I refuse to let myself be a victim of this.

Given all that has transpired in my life, playing the role of the victim would be incredibly easy for me to do. However, doing so neither benefits me nor inspires anyone else. It is up to me to let the experiences of the past teach me and give me the confidence I need in order to help other people.

The goal of this exercise is to take a negative experience from your past and figure out how you can turn it into something positive for the future.

June 26

> Be courteous to nerds because you never know when you could end up working for one.

Always extend to other people the same level of courtesy that you expect to receive yourself. You should never treat someone differently based on their socioeconomic rank or any other status, and you should never make assumptions about someone else's status.

On the other hand, under no circumstances should this be used as an excuse to discriminate against anyone. You should treat other people with kindness and love at all times.

It is important to remember to never look down on another person because if you do, you will one day find yourself doing the same thing to someone else. It doesn't matter which road you take to get there if you don't have a certain destination in mind.

June 27.

> It is less vital to have a certain destination in mind than it is to have the desire to develop yourself and to be open to the numerous possibilities that lay in wait for you.

As you continue to mature, that will undergo a change.

You should make it your mission to seize all opportunities that come your way by remaining open to new experiences.

Your goal is to be receptive to all opportunities!

June 28

> You never know when or where luck and good fortune will enter your life.

You can't hope that other people will love you in spite of your flaws and deficiencies if you don't love yourself despite those things about yourself.

It's possible that the aspect of our character that other people admire the most is also the trait that causes us the greatest inadequacy. It is not expected of you to have the same outward appearance as everyone else. Because we are all unique, it is important to accept and appreciate any imperfections or flaws that you may have because they are a part of who you are.

Goal: Be proud of your originality. You are one of a kind and cannot be compared to anyone else on earth.

June 29

> You should only keep company with people with whom you can converse.

Communication is a vital component of any kind of interaction. There are some people whose personalities simply do not complement yours in any way. It is not worth your time to investigate the reason. If you move to an area where you will be appreciated and needed, the rest of your life will fall into place.

Your mission is to make amends with anyone in your life with whom you are unable to form a meaningful connection by trying to do so. When you speak to them, make sure that the tone of your voice emanates love and respect for the other person. This will help you connect with them.

June 30

In order to fully embrace the life that is awaiting us, we must first let go of the life that we had imagined for ourselves.

It's wonderful to have ideas, plans, and goals, but it's important to remember that not all of them will be realized. You could end up being disappointed if you build elaborate scenarios in your head, so try to have an open mind and be prepared for things to change.

Accepting everything that life throws at you, no matter how challenging it may be, is the goal here.

Month July, Chapter 7

July 1

> Because our time here is limited, you should prioritize activities that bring you joy. There is not a moment to lose at this point.

I can still remember being five years old and having the ambition to become a famous person, specifically the next Shirley Temple. I was inspired to excel in singing, dancing, and acting because I fell in love with all three of those activities. I'm really thankful that I started having great dreams at such a young age because it allowed me to zero in on what it was that I truly wanted to accomplish. Whatever your age, you must pursue your desire until it is yours. You can't just wait around for your dreams to come true and expect them to start materializing. It is never going to be perfect, and it is unlikely that it will ever be exactly how you saw it. Nevertheless, you should pursue activities that bring you joy.

The goal is to stop putting off achieving a significant goal. Put in as much effort as possible to achieve it.

On July 2,

> When we meet guys, whose personalities are the opposite of our own, we should look at ourselves and figure out why.

When we find ourselves troubled by the actions or behaviors of other people, it is usually a mirror of something we are fighting with on the inside of ourselves. We have a propensity to view the challenges that another person is going through as a reflection of our own problems. We won't be able to project our problems onto other people if we are aware of them and, most importantly, address them internally. It's always interesting to go deeper and figure out what's bothering us as individuals. What we find is frequently surprising and fascinating in its own right.

What characteristic or quality of a close friend or member of your family has been driving you absolutely bonkers? Think about whether it might be more important to you than you thought at first, and then get to work on making it better.

July 3

> Every child is a developing artist in his or her own right. The challenge that he has is how to continue his artistic career as he gets older.

Keeping your sense of innocence, youth, and freedom is absolutely necessary if you want to experience happiness in your life. We all have the intrinsic power to create and shape our own lives, which makes us all artists. Keeping this in mind, it is extremely important to ensure that you never lose your sense of carefree wonder and remain curious about both yourself and the world around you.

The end goal is that maturing does not require you to give up the things that fascinate you in order to progress. Always be sure to schedule time in your schedule for the things you've always wanted to do.

July 4

> Because breaking free from one's own chains is just part of what it is to be free, one must also live in a way that acknowledges, honors, and encourages the independence of others.

Making sure that the people around you have the same level of physical and emotional liberty as you do is an important component of living a genuine and honest life. Even though we are fortunate to live in a free nation, there are still social injustices that occur on a daily basis, not just in the United States but also in other parts of the world. As caring members of the human race, it is our duty to do everything we can to help keep and strengthen the independence of the people around us.

Your freedom is a gift that should not be taken for granted; instead, celebrate it and encourage others to do the same.

July 5

> The best way to avoid being embarrassed is to be able to laugh at yourself when you do something embarrassing.

On more than one occasion, I've been known to trip and fall while performing. The truth is that over the course of my life, I've come to embrace and even enjoy the fact that I'm closure of my life, I've come to embrace and even enjoy the fact that I'm clumsy. Every time I trip and fall onstage, I have the choice of being embarrassed and running away or staying on my feet, smiling, and striking a pose. If I can make other people laugh before they laugh at me, then the decline won't be quite as painful.

Try to get a good laugh out of yourself. Don't put too much weight on what happens.

July 6

> For a mature woman, praying is not a frivolous way to pass the time. When it comes to acting, having a proper understanding of it and using it effectively is the most powerful instrument there is.

Many people have the misconception that praying must be an organized activity that takes place in a religious building like a church, synagogue, or mosque. When I pray, I speak to God as if he were my best friend. I address him as "you." I don't try to keep my feelings to myself, nor do I wait to be in a holy location before expressing them. I am aware that it is possible for people to hear me no matter where I am. Even if you don't believe in God, you should still pray to the cosmos, since doing so demonstrates that you are being truthful with yourself. It implies that you are open to change, learning, and receiving aid when you put your energy out into the world.

The purpose of this exercise is to pray to whoever or whatever you believe in and ask for guidance or understanding concerning anything that has been bothering you.

July 7

When we shift our focus from the challenges we face to the benefits we already have, everything in our lives begins to improve.

After completing therapy, I came to the realization that my way of thinking about a number of different topics needed to be modified. One of the most important adjustments I made was to concentrate more on what I did have than on what I did not. When I focused on the things and people in my life that I was grateful for and counted as blessings, I saw that more and more of those blessings and people began to show up in my regular life. When you start to visualize and keep powerful positive images in your head, it will seem almost miraculous to you. This is the power that comes from giving thanks.

Create a list of the top five people in your life with whom you can talk about anything and who will always have your back.

July 8

If you could change one thing about your life, what would it be? Enjoy yourself in the here and now.

Right now, as you sit here reading this, this is all you have. You already have everything you need to be happy right now: you, yourself, and your life. Because we spend so much time thinking about the past and the future, we often fail to appreciate how fortunate we are to be alive and to be surrounded by such wonderful things.

The goal is to pay attention to the experiences of the current moment. Appreciate the gift of life and the good fortune with which you were blessed to be born.

July 9

Absolutely no one deserves to be treated with anything other than adoration.

We have earned the right to experience many forms of love. People who were not shown love when they were young are the most likely to harbor hatred and are least deserving of it. It is up to each of us to make sure that we love the people around us as much as we love ourselves, and it is our responsibility to do so. People who give off the impression of being angry and toxic are not always the types of people you should spend time with, but you should at least try to think pleasant thoughts about them.

The goal is to be grateful for the capacity to experience, give, receive, and feel love for one another. It is a wonderful present.

July 10

If a person thinks that concepts such as peace and love are tired clichés that must have faded away in the 1960s, then that is his problem.

Love and peace are timeless qualities.

I frequently find myself wishing that I had been born in the 1960s because that was such a fantastic decade in terms of music, civil rights, fashion, politics, and culture. On the other hand, one of the most motivational parts of that time period was the peace movement. The sight of so many people, spanning multiple generations, coming together in support of love and peace is something that I find both uplifting and beautiful. I have faith and hope that we will be able to carry on living our lives with tolerance, kindness, compassion, and love for one another. Today, more than ever, it is critical for all of us to put these values into practice and raise awareness of them.

The goal of this endeavor is to spread the message of love and peace everywhere you go. Hugs should be given out for free today.

July the eleventh

Is today the day when the universe will open doors for you where there were previously only walls if you pursue your happiness?

In a world full of unknowns and challenges, I've found that the easiest rule of thumb for me to follow is to focus on activities that bring me joy. When you have the courage to consider every possibility, the world opens up in ways that you could never have imagined. Follow what makes you happy, and fantastic opportunities will present themselves to you.

Your goal is to concentrate on activities that provide you the most pleasure and happiness.

July 12

Crying takes away some of the pain and makes you feel better, while also washing away the pain.

Everyone, regardless of how powerful or tough they believe they are, is required to communicate their sentiments occasionally. Some people shed tears on a consistent basis, while others only do so on occasion. But I'm aware that when I have a genuine need to cry and finally give in to that desire, I feel like a completely different person. It's a way for me to express my pain as well as let go and let go of things.

The point is that it's bad for your health to bottle up strong feelings; therefore, you should let them out.

The 13th of July

> A dream is the only thing that keeps a sleeping man company.

If you don't put in the effort to get what you want, your goals and ambitions will never be realized. You can't just give up and expect everything to work out for the best. People who help themselves are more likely to be successful in life, and God helps those who help themselves.

We all have a purpose; thus, you should make sure that you are moving in the direction of your goals.

14 July

> Go ahead and carry it out. Come to a stop on the ground. When viewed from below, the globe takes on a quite distinct appearance.

Failure, making mistakes, gaining new knowledge, and starting over are all-natural occurrences in human existence. If I had regarded the fact that I need treatment as an indication of my inadequacy, I wouldn't be where I am now. Instead, I decided to start over, face my problems, and work my way back up to where I was before.

Believe me when I say it wasn't simple. At times, it would have been simple for me to give up and stay in the same place I was. On the other hand, there are times when we have to hit rock bottom before we can see the way out. Our shortcomings do not determine who we are; rather, they shape us, and as a result, we are stronger.

Consider how the lessons you've learned from your past mistakes have helped you become a better person.

July 15

> Being grateful is the key to finding happiness.

I will be forever grateful to all of my friends, family, and fans who have been there for me while I work through the process of getting better. I will be forever thankful to everyone who has advocated on my behalf, since doing so has provided me with the strength that I required to break out of this situation and get started on the road to healing.

Aim: Make it a priority to express gratitude to everyone in your life for being there for you today, paying special attention to those who have stood by your side during challenging times.

July 16

> You should never feel guilty for the fact that you are still alive.

People have a habit of apologizing for things for which they have no reason to do so, which happens far too frequently. We are all responsible for it. Even if it wasn't our fault, we always apologize if we startle someone or accidentally bump into another person.

We aren't attempting to be anything other than polite. However, you are essentially telling yourself that you do not have the qualifications necessary to occupy the position that you currently have. You have worked hard and deserve to be where you are on this earth, wherever that may be.

Aim: You should be pleased with where you are right now and with how far you have come along your route. You are exactly where you ought to be at this point.

July 17

> There are instances when you have no choice but to lie. On the other hand, you should always be honest with yourself.

If you make a mistake, you shouldn't beat yourself up over it because it already occurred and there's no way for you to fix it by going back in time. Nevertheless, you have committed an error in judgment if you are not honest with yourself about the mistake you have made. Even though we are all just going through the motions of life and picking up lessons as we go, it is essential to acknowledge when you have done something wrong, even if it was unintentional. Simply apologizing, accepting responsibility, moving on, and putting the past behind you will set you free.

Apologize to someone for a recent error, whether it was a major or tiny mistake. This is the goal.

July 18

> Always carry yourself as though you are wearing a crown, even if it is only in your mind.

When we give such a large portion of ourselves to our work, it is essential that we do well in our jobs. It is essential to give credit to your hard work and creative endeavors, regardless of what other people think of the products you produce. When we put in the effort and get the necessary expertise, our creative abilities typically improve. You can generally expect each job you take on to be more satisfying than the one that came before it. It is not about being perfect; instead, the focus should be on getting better.

Remember to give yourself credit for all of the effort, devotion, and creativity you've put in, no matter how you feel about it.

The 19th of July

> Do not give in to your worries; if you do, you will find that you are unable to communicate with your feelings.

Love sheds light on everything, whereas fear clouds your perception of the truth and causes you to dwell on unfavorable thoughts. When you're scared, you can take cover behind your chest. Fear grips the entire population. It takes a lot of courage to face your worries and do what your heart tells you to do.

Focus on listening to your gut instincts and paying attention to your heart.

July 20

> When it comes to life, you get what you have the courage to ask for.

Your life will be filled with people who enter and then leave it. You shouldn't expect everyone to know how to make you happy, so you shouldn't waste your time worrying about it; just let it go. The people who remain in your life are the ones who contribute to the positive emotions you experience. However, you should not put your happiness in the hands of other people because there is a good chance that you will be let down on occasion.

If you have been disappointed by another person, your goal should be to ask yourself, "Will this matter a year from now?" It will make it easier for you to let go of the past and gain some perspective.

The 21st of July

> Every person has his or her own problems that most people don't know about, and we often call a man "cold" when he's just sad.

There is no reason to take anything personally. Anything that other people say or do is a mirror of how they are truly feeling on the inside, not of you personally. People are kind and loving to you because they are kind and loving to themselves, and this reflects in their interactions with you. People will lash out at you verbally and physically not because you have done anything wrong, but rather because they are going through a difficult time of their own. Have sympathy for people who choose to act aggressively toward others. We have no idea what difficulties they are facing back at home.

Imagine that if someone tries to hurt you in the future, it is like a drop of water that just slides off of you like a bead of water.

The 22nd of July

> All that youngsters require is a little assistance, a little hope, and the support of an individual who has faith in them.

Instilling hope in the hearts of young people is a priceless gift. A significant number of children are raised in broken homes, where they are deprived of affection, emotional sustenance, and support. When you give a child hope, they will see all of the opportunities available to them.

Aim: to step outside of your comfort zone by volunteering with children who are less fortunate than you.

The 23rd of July

> Nothing can be changed until it is confronted, but nothing can be changed until it is challenged.

My life has been profoundly affected by bullying, which has resulted in significant harm. For a very long time, I let the pain determine who I was as a person. It was essential for me to find a middle ground between taking everything in and letting go of my attachments. When I stood up to the bully, I took a tremendous leap forward in my development. I told her how her comments had left me feeling broken and helpless and how they were her fault. They eventually brought on more mental and physical issues, which I am currently attempting to address and manage. She had a difficult time recalling the things she had done, and she was certain that now that I had achieved success, I would have forgotten everything. I was stunned by the divergent points of view that you and I held, but more than anything else, I felt as though a massive burden had been removed from my shoulders. I was able to find the power and clarity I required after forgiving her, which was exactly what I required all along.

Take into consideration a person from your past who has caused you damage. Think of their shortcomings with compassion.

July 24

> It is far easier to avoid developing bad habits than it is to break bad ones.

It is time to stop engaging in destructive activities. They are doing nothing more than getting in the way of your recovery. Sometimes we fail to recognize the negative effects that our unhealthy actions are having on us. We are nervous about releasing them into the world, but now is the right time to do it.

Goal: Create a list of the ways in which you behave. Are you feeling better as a result of being with them?

July 25

> In the end, everything will turn out OK; if it doesn't, then it isn't the end yet.

When you are going through a difficult time, you may feel as though your life is over and that it is a complete and utter loss. Nevertheless, you are not even in the vicinity. When I first started going to therapy, I was under the impression that my life was over. I was concerned that I wouldn't be able to find work and that fewer people would appreciate me for who I am. I was under the impression that the world was coming to an end, but in reality, it was the first day of the rest of my life. No matter what you are going through, you always have the option to start over, and doing so can provide you with hope.

The goal is to give yourself enough time to process everything that is going on in your life right now.

July 26

There is never a time when it is too late to begin again. You have an unbounded amount of enthusiasm.

When you connect with your passion, there are no limits to what you can accomplish. Passion is the engine that drives the creation of any form of art, and it is up to you to make something beautiful with your life.

Your goal should be to keep in mind that if you put in a lot of work, you can accomplish amazing things.

July 27

Put forth an effort to make the world a more pleasant place for everyone.

I have a great commitment to making the world a better place for those who will live on it in the future. Being a public figure has opened up many wonderful doors for me, including opportunities to volunteer my time and make a positive difference in the lives of a huge number of other people. Around the world, I have had the privilege of serving as an advocate for children and people who are struggling with issues related to bullying, eating disorders, and mental health. Everyone has problems that are close to their hearts; thus, you should act to make a difference in any field you are particularly interested in. To donate your time, pick up the phone and give a local nonprofit organization a call.

July 28

To achieve success, you must be authentic in all you do.

One of the most difficult challenges one faces in life is figuring out who they are meant to be. If you're already well on your way to being who you want to be, consider yourself a success simply because you've advanced further than the majority of people.

Aim: To be of assistance to a friend who is feeling disoriented. They might benefit from your assistance in developing their individual identities.

July 29

Because no one is as powerful as they appear, you should just be yourself.

At some point in our lives, the vast majority of us have resorted to hiding behind our preferred mythology or fictitious character. For me, that character has always been Cinderella. She is forced into service and forced to live in the shadow of her sisters until her unfortunate circumstances change for the better one day. When I was younger, people frequently referred to me as being Dallas Lovato's younger sister. I was always under her shadow, despite the fact that she never intended for me to feel this way about it. I was proud to be able to call her my sister, but I never got the sense that I could show my true potential around her. It has taken a lot of work for me to get to the point where I am confident in my own skills. I am aware that overcoming that obstacle was an essential step that needed to be taken in order for me to get to the point where I can say that I truly enjoy myself. Since I stopped being angry at my sister, I can now get along better with her.

The goal is to never be content with living in the shadow of another person. Get out there and learn to love the person you are.

July 30

> Always have an optimistic outlook. The most wonderful sensation in the world is the realization that one's options are not limited in any way.

Even in the darkest moments of our lives, there is always a sliver of light and a speck of hope that may be unearthed. Grab hold of that optimism and allow the exhilaration of all the possibilities to be the engine that drives you forward.

When you're feeling sad, you should look within for a glimmer of hope, and then you should allow your mind to wander freely with the possibility of what's to come.

July 31

> Even this will pass at some point.

When I think back on some of the horrible situations I've had in my life, I realize how difficult it may be to triumph over hopelessness and pain. I am aware that time does not completely remove scars, but it does help to ease the agony that is associated with them. No matter how long it takes, you will ultimately start to feel better after this. You'll come to terms with what's transpired.

Aim: No matter how you're feeling right now, remind yourself that things will get better in the future, and let that knowledge bring you joy in the meanwhile. It is going to get better.

Month August, Chapter 8

August 1

> **With optimism, there is no obstacle that cannot be overcome.**

Throughout my life, I've had multiple experiences in which I've been disoriented, broken, confused, and wracked with agony. The ups and downs of my life have shown me the importance of maintaining my faith at all times. I am confident that as long as I continue to have hope and trust in the future, I will be fine no matter what.

Objective: Recall a time in your life when you felt like there was no hope and think about how you got through it. Make use of it for upcoming challenges. You are able to triumph over any challenge that you face.

August 2

> **Love is the answer, and you are aware of this fact; love is a flower, and you need to give it the space to blossom.**

Love and respect are essential components of any successful partnership. These things require some amount of time. Put forth the effort to strengthen the connection you have with yourself in addition to the connections you have with your family and friends. Simply letting someone know that you love them is not enough. You have to put in the time and effort to demonstrate your love through the things that you say and do.

The objective is to communicate your concern for another person through the actions you take. It's not always enough to just say the words "I love you."

August 3

It takes courage to grow up and become the person you were always meant to be.

The process of maturing is difficult, and just when we think we've reached the end of it, we discover that we've only just begun. When I started going to therapy, I foolishly believed that all of my problems were solved. The truth is that you need to consistently put effort into bettering yourself and your recovery. Moving forward and being willing to accept change takes a lot of guts since it is quite easy for us to become too comfortable.

Conquer any obstacles that stand in your way so that you can develop into the person you were always meant to be.

August 4

For every action, there is an equal and opposite reaction.

After the passing of my father, I was completely struck with a profound feeling of grief and sadness. Despite all of my misery, I came to realize that there was also hope. I had to acknowledge how I felt and use those feelings to do something good.

My relationship with my father was strained due to the fact that he struggled with both mental illness and addiction. As a result of this, I decided to honor him by establishing the Lovato Scholarship at Cast Recovery. This scholarship will provide financial assistance to one individual at a time who is battling an addiction or mental health condition. This was my plan for turning a bad thing that happened to me into something good and rewarding.

The next time you find yourself in a difficult situation, your goal should be to look for a way to improve it and discover a way out.

August 5

> We are the sum of all the things we do, so greatness is a pattern, not a single thing.

Any talent that you wish to become an expert in requires both patience and consistent practice. It is as simple as brushing our teeth, which is something we do so frequently that we hardly give it a second thought. By doing something on a consistent basis, we can turn a positive behavior into a routine aspect of our life. It's important to form good habits, and the more of them you have, the better off you'll be in the long run. When you try to improve yourself on a daily basis, you will eventually succeed.

You should make it a habit to engage in activities that you enjoy and that are helpful to you.

August 6

> We must continue to live regardless of how many heavens have collapsed.

Don't try to fight the natural order of things; everything happens for a reason and at the correct moment. Surrender to these blessings, as well as your challenges, with grace and ease.

The objective is to give in to whatever it is that you're struggling with today.

The seventh of August

> I am not a fan of gambling, but if there is one thing on which I am willing to gamble my reputation, it is myself.

The process of recovery was a humiliating ordeal for me, but it taught me things about myself that I could never have anticipated learning. My freedom comes from understanding and embracing the fact that I will never reach perfection. It is imperative that I continue putting in significant effort toward my recovery, as it is a process that occurs on a daily basis. I can't afford to get complacent or take things for granted, but I suppose that's all part of the educational process.

Think about your path and the ways you can continue to enrich and improve your life every day, even if you are not in the process of getting better.

August 8

> The purpose of the journey of discovery is not to look for new sights but rather to train one's eyes to see things in a different way.

It is essential to have an open mind when interacting with the outside world. Even in the most routine of settings, you should always keep an eye out for anything new that might have occurred. It's a fantastic thing to see the world, but it's a waste of time if you're not willing to try new things along the way.

The goal of this exercise is to look at something or someone in a different way. Let go of any ideas or beliefs you have about the situation.

August 9

> Keep in mind that only God has the right to judge you. Put the naysayers out of your mind; you have supporters.

It is not possible to please every single person. The only thing that truly deserves your attention is how you choose to live your life. Keep in mind that another people's disapproval doesn't say anything about you as a person, and say what you want to say even if they don't like it.

Avoid giving any thought to how other people will see you or how you will express yourself. This is the goal. As long as you are working to improve yourself and bring happiness to yourself, nothing else really matters.

August the tenth

> If you want to make it in this world, you have to learn how to communicate with other people.

Once you have mastered how to communicate with other people, there is no problem that you will not be able to solve. It does not indicate that you will always agree with other people, nor does it imply that other people will always agree with you. Nor does it imply that you will always agree with them. But none of this matter unless you possess the maturity and patience to work through the differences you have with others. Think about how much more peace there would be on our planet if people would just talk things out instead of resorting to violence when they couldn't figure out how to solve a problem.

Do you have a close friend or member of your family with whom you sometimes find it challenging to communicate? Perhaps it's time to give it another shot. There is no downside to trying something new.

The 11th of August

> It is not your place to pass judgment on other people, therefore do not waste your time or energy doing so.

It is not within your purview to do so.

You were not brought to this location to pass judgment on the other people who are here. You have developed into the most improved version of yourself that is even imaginable, and you radiate love to everyone you come into contact with.

It is important to refrain from passing judgment on other individuals and instead direct one's energy toward creating a positive impact on the world. This is the goal.

The 12th of August

> In order to cohabit happily, we need to spend more time getting to know one another.

Because the space on this planet is shared by all of us, developing mutual respect is necessary for coexistence. We don't have to be in complete accord on everything, but we do need to accept and acknowledge both our similarities and our differences.

Reach out to a new friend, roommate, or coworker and try to get to know them better so you can have a better relationship with them. It's possible that you'll be surprised by how much information you share or how moved people are by your efforts.

The 13th of August

> Those who cause others the most pain are often the ones who have to go through it themselves.

When I was a child and was subjected to bullying, I remember being incensed by the way other people treated me. Now I see that those other people were going through the same kind of pain that I was, albeit in a different way. Now I see that those other people were going through the same kind of pain that I was, albeit in a different way. When I think of the people who bullied me in the past, it makes me want to give them a hug because I know that at the time, they needed love and compassion.

Consider at least one person who has caused you pain in the past. This is your goal. Show them some compassion because it was obvious that they were going through a painful experience.

August 14

People learn how to treat you based on what you tolerate, what you prohibit, and what you reinforce in their behavior toward you.

Remember that not everyone is an extrovert by nature, even if you are someone who is naturally outgoing. Everyone here ought to show consideration for other people and their individual tastes. Always be aware of the limits that other people set for themselves. Tell the person who is stepping on your toes that they need to be more respectful of them if they continue. People have attempted to pull me in many directions throughout my life, and there have been occasions when I've had to put up boundaries or get away from certain situations.

The goal is to be conscious of and sensitive to the limitations that others have. It is not reasonable to assume that another person will feel at ease if you behave in a particular manner simply because you do.

August 15

Have compassion for everyone, regardless of their financial situation; this is a difficult time for everyone.

The amount of suffering that some people go through is disproportionate to the amount that others go through.

When we compare our woes to those of other people, we frequently end up feeling guilty and inadvertently invalidate our own experiences in the process. It wasn't until I broke my ankle that I realized that there are people on the other side of the world who don't even have access to clean water. It wasn't until I broke my ankle that I realized that there are people on the other side of the world who don't even have access to clean water. Although there may be someone else who is going through a more severe ordeal than we are, it is important not to assign blame to ourselves since it is important to acknowledge that all suffering is real. Also, the fact that you did not have as much as someone else does not mean that you were spared the pain of the situation.

No matter what you are going through, the point is to acknowledge and validate what you are now experiencing. Regarding your emotions as if they were those of another person, recognize and appreciate them.

August 16

You aren't helping yourself when you compare yourself to others in any way, shape, or form.

The fact that no two people are identical is what distinguishes each of us from one another and explains why we are all so remarkable. It is in our nature to evaluate ourselves as well as others, and when we are uncomfortable, we start making comparisons between ourselves and other people. We take into consideration if someone is more attractive or skilled than us, as well as whether someone has more money than us. However, this is irrelevant since you are not that person, nor will you ever be that person. You are perfect in every way because that is exactly how God envisioned you.

The objective is to keep in mind that no one else on this earth has the same heart as you do, and that fact alone is something that should be treasured.

August 17

Give yourself permission to feel all of your feelings, even those that are unpleasant, such as dread. Just keep going, because there is no feeling that can truly define you.

When we are completely submerged in a certain feeling, we tend to have the mistaken belief that it will last forever. The key is to not fight against that emotion, since doing so will only make your anguish and suffering worse in the long run. We are given the opportunity to live in this world so that we might feel a diverse range of emotions, such as joy and sadness, laughter and gloom. Because you can't influence the way you feel in every situation, the best strategy is to just let your emotions flow freely and understand that they won't last forever.

Keep in mind that pain is an inevitable component of the human experience. It enables us to appreciate the good times that much more when they come.

August 18th

> You can either run with or be run by the day.

When you wake up in a bad mood, it seems to color your entire day, and if you don't catch it in time, you will begin to feel as if your entire day is doomed to fail. If you don't catch it in time, you will feel as if your entire day is doomed. Believe it or not, you have the power to shift your mindset and make the decision to not let a single negative thought or experience ruin your entire day. I'm not going to pretend that it's always simple, because I'm well aware of how challenging it sometimes is. Give it a shot and see how much joy and light you can bring into the world with it.

The goal for today is to put the laws of attraction into practice. No matter what happens, you should always keep sending out positive energy to the cosmos and then observe what the universe sends back to you.

August 19

> perform mundane tasks with a great deal of affection.

If you give everything you do in life 100 percent of your heart, the impact you have on the world will be far larger than you could have ever imagined.

The goal is to give even the most menial of responsibilities the complete attention they deserve. Even something as simple as giving someone a hug or saying "thank you" ought to be accorded the same level of respect and focus as more substantial acts of kindness.

August 20

> Even miracles require some amount of time.

When we were younger, we had the naive belief that all of our wishes might be accomplished with the flick of a wrist or the point of a finger. It is not to say that beautiful things can't happen quickly, but in most cases, remarkable things require a period of time to unfold.

I have no doubt in my mind that miraculous occurrences are feasible. Because of your belief in me, I am provided with the fortitude to keep being strong.

The end game requires patience. Even the most significant shifts in our lives require some settling time.

August 21

> You have no financial obligations to anyone else but yourself. Set aside some time for your own needs.

Be respectful of both yourself and the area you occupy. Establish limits.

A significant number of the lessons I've picked up have to do with standing up for myself and imposing boundaries on my behavior. It's extremely difficult, even painful at times. Establish boundaries with the people you spend time with, both at work and in your everyday life, and stick to them. Check to see if they are aware of your preferences and the limitations you face. Act and engage in conversation with other people so that you can be confident that you are respecting yourself. It's not easy, but it's definitely worth the effort.

The goal for today is to set up at least one barrier in either your professional or personal life.

August 22

Because of my mother, I've never given much thought to the question of whether or not I'm a particularly bright person. Consideration of the matter is completely pointless.

You could spend your entire life worrying about what other people think of you, but then you would have wasted all of that time and energy worrying about things that are out of your control. It is of no consequence to worry about what other people think of you. It is impossible to please everyone, and achieving that goal is not the purpose for which we were put on this earth. The most important thing is to be able to go to sleep each night with the knowledge that you gave it your all and conducted yourself with love, honesty, and compassion toward both other people and yourself.

Your objective is to make the most of each day by focusing your attention not on meaningless matters that are beyond your control or that will take over your life, but on those things that truly matter.

August 23

Identify both your purpose and your unique voice.

There is a reason for each and every one of us to be here on earth. When we are very young, some of us already know what we want to do with our lives, while others may need more time to figure themselves out. Regardless of when you discover it, you are already on this planet to carry out a certain assignment. Your tone is unique and absolutely beautiful. When you find something that makes you happy, make sure to embrace it, and never let someone convince you that you can't achieve the things you set out to do.

Create a list of everything you want to accomplish in your lifetime as your goal. There is no bearing on the grandiosity of the dream; in fact, the more expansive it is, the better.

August 24

> Have no regrets, and live your life to the fullest.

Nobody is faultless. In addition to this, it is necessary to be able to forgive oneself. Do not ruminate on the mistakes you have made in the past. The more you focus your attention on it and hold onto it, the more vitality and power it will acquire. As a consequence of this, you should let it go, take what you can from it, and go on.

The objective is to forgive yourself for a mistake you've made or an action you've taken that you now feel bad about. Give yourself permission to let it go.

August 25

> In the end, only three things matter: how profoundly you loved, how carefully you lived, and how gracefully you let go of things that were never meant for you.

Why do we waste so much time worrying about the one thing we didn't obtain when our lives are filled with so many beautiful things? Think about the possibility that the one thing you wanted so much but couldn't get was never really meant for you to have it in the first place. Instead, take some time to acknowledge and be grateful for the love and gifts that are currently in your life.

The objective of this exercise is to think of something that you desired but did not have and that ultimately turned out to be a blessing in disguise.

August 26

When you give it your all and work toward achieving your objectives, you inspire other people to do the same.

The more effort you put into making your goals a reality, the more positive energy you will be able to share with those around you. Others will gain the self-assurance, motivation, and freedom to pursue their own aspirations if they see that you have the guts to go for yours.

You are a living demonstration of something that many people believe to be impossible. There is no present that you could give to someone that would be more thoughtful than this.

The goal is for you to spend time with a friend who is determined, and if you're feeling uninspired or worried about pursuing your goals, you can draw motivation from them.

August 27

Adhere to honesty and loyalty as your first set of guiding principles.

Sincerity and faithfulness are two of the most fundamental principles that guide one's life. Without these guiding principles, life on this planet would have no point. I make it a point to be truthful with myself, my friends, my family, and my followers on a daily basis.

What are the most important things to you? Make sure that the way you go about your daily life is in line with the values and beliefs that guide your life.

August 28

> If you lack bravery, there is nothing in this world that you will ever be able to accomplish. The mental quality is thought to be the second most important thing after honor.

We give ourselves much too little credit for all of the inner strength that we possess. Some people might have more than others, yet in the end, even if you tried but were unsuccessful, you would still be considered a winner. You tried, which demonstrates more bravery than anything else you could ever do.

The goal for today is to give everything you've got to whatever you choose to do.

August 29

> You could spend minutes, hours, days, weeks, or even months overanalyzing a situation, attempting to piece together the jigsaw puzzle and reasoning what could've, would've happened... or you could just leave the pieces on the floor and carry on with your life.

If you allow yourself to spend your days and thoughts concentrating on the past, you will eventually come to the realization that you are unhappy. This is because you are missing all of the wonder and excitement that the present has to offer. Focus your attention solely on the here and now. Remember to focus on your breathing and express gratitude for the current situation. When the source of our joy is there in front of us, we have a propensity to dwell on the pleasures of the past and the prospects of the future.

Objective: If you dwell too much on the past, it will be impossible for you to enjoy life in the here and now. Today is the day to work on improvement.

August 30

> Your time is valuable, so avoid wasting it by pretending to lead the life of another person.

As I progressed in my work as an artist, I found that the amount of success I had was a good indicator of how much I enjoyed life. But as I continued my journey along this road, I became aware of how many hills and valleys there were. If I allow the thoughts and perspectives of other people to determine who I am, I will never be satisfied with who I am. I am very thankful that I can handle the highs and lows in my life because I have the resilience and the capacity to love myself.

The objective is to discover your own power by cultivating love for yourself. Also, don't let the opinions of other people shape who you are.

August 31

> Give what you would like to receive. If you want to be happy, you need to make other people happy.

According to the fundamental principle of attraction, the universe will give you exactly what you send out into the universe. More love will be returned to you in proportion to the amount of love you give. When you let more love into your life, the universe will shower you with even more love in return. When we give positive energy to the world, we are rewarded with a lovely feeling. We bring joy to those who are closest to us.

Your mission is to set a shining example of each and every value and principle that you hold dear.

Month September, Chapter 9

September 1

I don't require anything else to complete me because I'm already stunning and deserving.

When we truly feel complete on the inside, that is when we can claim ownership of our inner beauty and power. Every one of us is unique in both the things that can make us happy and the ways in which we wish to live our lives. These criteria are formed and shaped by our own personal experiences of learning via trial and error. Adapting to new circumstances and expanding our operations require that we regularly develop and adjust these standards. If you stay true to your innermost self and your voice, you'll never feel like anything is missing from your life.

Today, remind yourself that you do not require the help of another person to be whole because you are already whole in and of yourself.

September 2

Your soul will awaken when it experiences love, because love awakens it.

It is possible for us to repress our actual feelings, whether they are sad, glad, or romantic, if we are subjected to negative influences such as gossip, judgments, bullying, and other similar behaviors. It is challenging to believe that you can be yourself even when you are surrounded by people who love you. As you open up your heart and soul to the love of those around you, you will feel an incredible surge of joy.

Aim: Make it a point to express gratitude to those in your life who love and accept you just as you are.

September 3

> Yesterday is gone, tomorrow is unknowable, but today is a gift from the present. Because of this, we talk about it being in the "present."

Because nobody knows how long we are going to be here, you shouldn't waste your time worrying about the future while we are here. You really want to just relish the moment and try to treasure it as much as you possibly can.

The goal is to acknowledge that time is limited and to challenge yourself to seize each day's opportunities to the fullest. What steps can you take now to ensure that you are making the most of every moment of your life?

September 4

> God did not make it necessary for me to find him; rather, he has always been there. Even if they succeed in imprisoning me, the walls of the prison will never be able to hold my spirit or my love.

In conclusion, your spirit and your soul should never, ever be bargained away. No matter what limitations or restrictions other people try to impose on you, the ability to love both yourself and other people is the force that moves mountains.

The goal here is to not let the constraints of your emotions hold you back.

The fifth of September

> What a beautiful life... You have earned the right to have it.

Never undervalue what you bring to the table. Never forget how lovely you are. People in certain contexts have the potential to routinely give us the impression that we do not measure up to society's expectations.

It's natural for you to have those feelings. You just need to know how to get yourself out of that dangerous situation.

The objective is to convince yourself that you are beautiful without making any changes to who you are.

September 6

> At the break of each new day, we are renewed. The action that we take right now is the most significant factor.

Because we are reborn each day, there is no way that we can ever be doomed because life is always full of new opportunities. You could wake up one day and make the decision to switch occupations, travel the world, or get in touch with an old friend you haven't talked to in years. New ideas and possibilities await discovery with each passing day.

The objective for today is to engage in an activity that is not typical of you and is completely out of character. Free yourself from your chains.

7 September

> not based on appearances but on faith.

If I had only allowed myself to dream and live based on what I could see right in front of me, I never would have achieved the success that has brought me here today. But I had faith in the power of my dreams, my imagination, the strength of my ideas, and the hopes I had for a more fulfilling existence. It would have been easy for me to let the way I was treated at school—including being bullied and having harsh things shouted at me—determine how I lived my life, but I chose not to. Instead of choosing the life that was there in front of me, I decided to put my faith in the fact that my goals would carry me through the challenging times and eventually bring me to the place where I wanted to be.

What do you consider to be your most important goal? Say it aloud to yourself and convince yourself that the answer is there in front of you if you have faith in both the answer and in yourself.

September 8

One of the main reasons I was unhappy for so long was that I didn't want to acknowledge and accept my feelings for so long.

I didn't realize it at the time, but in my frenetic effort to keep control of my life, I was losing more and more of who I was as a person. I didn't grasp this at the time. My addictions gave me the impression that I was in control of my life. I was in over my head, and I couldn't see that I was becoming more and more detached from who I was. I was holding on to a great deal of suffering while using my addictions to dull the pain. When I initially started going to therapy, I felt completely out of control because I could no longer hide behind anything, and I hated that feeling. I had nothing to protect me. I was oblivious to the fact that I needed to cede authority to a more powerful entity. Now that I have everything out in the open and have asked for the help that I required, I am filled with immense gratitude.

Instead of saying that everything is alright when someone asks how you are, be honest with them about how you truly feel.

September 9

Trying to please everyone is a surefire way to fall short of your goals, which is why I don't know what the key to success is.

When you put effort into impressing other people, you frequently end up failing to impress yourself, whether or not you are aware of this fact. Do not alter who you are for anyone, regardless of your age or whether you are still coming of age or are an adult who is secure in who you are.

The objective is to focus on living for oneself, with the expectation that the rest will take care of itself when the time is right.

September 10

> Make a brilliant move, and others might follow in your footsteps.

However, for some reason, some people feel the need to ask for permission before doing something positive. Some people may be reluctant to step outside of their comfort zones and engage in activities that cause them to feel uneasy because of the fear of the unknown. People tend to act like the people they watch, so it's important to be a good example for the people in your immediate area.

The goal is to lead and inspire others through the good acts you perform.

September 11

> If either you or I have even a single idea of using violence or hatred against anyone else anywhere in the world right now, we are contributing to the number of people who are injured around the world.

The shedding of blood is a band-aid solution that just invites further bloodshed. In the world that we live in, we require people who are willing to find solutions through means of peace, conversation, honesty, and diplomacy. Although it can appear impossible to achieve, peace around the world is something that should be pursued.

The goal is to demonstrate that one does not need to be a politician in order to work toward the promotion of peace and the resolution of disputes. Be sure that every word you speak and every action you take comes from a place of love and that this is the foundation for everything you do.

September 12

> It doesn't matter if you're right or wrong; the other person still has a viewpoint.

No matter how convinced you are that you are in the "right" in a given situation, there is a good chance that the person with whom you are debating or disagreeing is just as convinced that they are in the right. Disputes frequently become more difficult to resolve since there is no one answer or solution that is always correct. Because there are two perspectives on the issue, it is essential to be aware of both of them before deciding.

The goal is to keep an open mind and be ready to listen to the perspective of the other person at all times. They might bring something to your attention that you hadn't considered before that is beneficial to your growth and could help you develop it.

13 September

> If you want to avoid making a mistake in the future, you should disclose the truth right now.

I believe that it is human nature for each and every one of us to have, at some point in our lives, told a number of lies, both big and small. Even if you only lied once, you should admit your mistake as soon as possible, explain what happened, and ask for forgiveness.

The goal for today is to not tell any lies, no matter how small.

September 14

> There is nothing more charming and appealing than a person who is confident in who they are and what they provide to the world.

It's quite attractive when someone knows exactly who they are and doesn't make any effort to disguise it from others. When a man or a woman walks into a room, the air is instantly charged with an air of assurance. The truth is that outer beauty can fade over time, but inner beauty, elegance, and a healthy love of oneself can last a lifetime, but only if they are cultivated.

The objective is to unearth your inner confidence and display it with pride.

15 September

> It is none of my business what other people think of me. It is none of their business either.

You could waste the entire day worrying about what other people think of you, and at some point, in our lives, each of us has been in that position. Everyone has an opinion, but it's not really vital to pay attention to what other people think because the choices you make with your life shouldn't be determined by what they think. Your organization is entirely under your control. When you allow the ideas and ideals of other people to define how you should live your life, that life is no longer yours to own and control.

The goal is to take criticism in a constructive way and not let other people's ideas change you.

September 16

> Your friends define you.

I came to the realization that the people with whom I chose to surround myself were direct reflections of myself. I came to the realization that even if they were high and I was clean, a small part of me still desired to have a relationship with them as friends. I had no choice but to come to terms with the fact that I could not have friends among those who were still struggling with the effects of their sickness. It was necessary to cut certain people out of my life since they were a negative influence on me. Since I am now on the path to recovery, I make it a point to surround myself with people who are upbeat and have strong principles.

The question at hand is, "What characteristics do you search for in a friend?" Create a list of the qualities and characteristics that are important to you, and then check to see if the people you associate with meet that criteria.

September 17

> You do not have to look like everyone else. Learn to accept yourself just as you are.

No matter who we are, everyone has days in their lives when they experience feelings of unease. The single most important thing to keep in mind is that we have all been through days like these before. After we have come to terms with that sensation, and only then, will we be able to experience it and move on with the rest of our lives.

When you're feeling anxious, look in the mirror and tell yourself reassuring things. This will help you feel more at ease.

September 18

> Until you actually do something, nothing will work.

In order to bring the finest version of who you are to whatever it is that you are doing, you need to be performing at the top of your game. This involves getting the recommended amount of sleep, eating a healthy diet, engaging in physical activity, practicing meditation, and taking care of your mind, body, and spirit. There are times when we fool ourselves into thinking that in order to demonstrate how hard we work, we have to push ourselves to the point of exhaustion. However, I can promise you that it is far preferable to establish a happy medium. You'll be happier and more productive, and the quality of your work will get better as a whole.

Examine your life to see if there is a sense of harmony across all domains and aspects of it.

September 19

> The only thing that comes from having expectations is the fear of being disappointed.

When we sit around doing nothing but waiting for things to take place, we are not truly living in the moment. We prepare ourselves to be let down, and then, when we do let ourselves down, we end up blaming ourselves, which just makes us feel worse. It is essential to have a clear vision of your life goals. At the same time, it is extremely important to maintain an open mind on the means by which and the settings in which those goals will be accomplished. The problem with anticipation is that it makes our expectations far more ambitious than they should be. Dreamers are incredible, but they also need to be realistic and based in reality.

The objective is to let go of your expectations, be open to the journey, and discover what is immediately in front of you.

The twentieth day of September

> Yet none of the colors I am composed of have fully materialized yet.

Creating works of art is only one aspect of what it means to be creative. Additionally, it enables you to purge toxic thoughts and feelings in a way that is productive and conducive to good health. For me, it's singing and playing different kinds of music. When I am performing, I am able to communicate my emotions without engaging in behaviors that are harmful to myself. Find a hobby that you are passionate about and that allows you to express yourself in a positive way.

September 21

Keep in mind that the fact that you did not acquire what you desired can actually be a huge blessing.

In my life, there have been a lot of instances in which I have not received what I desired or what I believed would be beneficial to me. I can see clearly today that the things that I previously believed were essential for me were, in fact, not what I required at all. Be humble enough to let go of your frustrations and acknowledge that it's possible that this turn of events is for the best, even if you don't comprehend what's going on right now.

Objective: To reflect on the ways in which early setbacks turned out to be blessings.

September 22

We are never different ages on the inside.

Do you remember how much fun it was when you were a kid? playing around in the great outdoors with your friends and not giving a care in the world? Just because we are getting older does not mean that we have to abandon our childlike qualities. There is a part of you that will always remain innocent and childlike. Even though they do not have the ability to make decisions any longer, they should still be able to take part in the activity and enjoy it.

In whatever you do, keep in mind the importance of appreciating the work that you perform and having fun.

September 23rd

You are the only individual on the face of the earth who comprehends how you should go about living your life.

If someone tries to convince you otherwise, it's because they're struggling to navigate the challenges of their own life and have concluded that it's easier to direct the lives of others. They are scared of their own reality, but you can help them if you show them how you live your life with conviction and courage by showing them how you live your own life.

The objective is to come to terms with your life in its current state, with all of its shortcomings and achievements, hopes and heartbreaks. Show that you trust and believe in your own life, and you will encourage others to live their own lives in a more present and full way. Be a model for others to follow.

September 24

Sometimes our own light begins to dim, and it is another person's flame that helps to rekindle it. Every one of us has a reason to be thankful to the people who were responsible for lighting the spark that was already present within us.

It is only natural that we are unable to maintain a positive and happy attitude 365 days out of the year. Our luminosity can be as dazzling as the sun at times, and at other times it can be a little less dazzling. It is essential to surround oneself with people who love one completely and unreservedly.

When we feel as though there is no longer any chance of success, we consult with these individuals. Genuine friends bring light into our lives and rekindle the flame of faith that sometimes flickers within us.

If you're having a bad day, you should surround yourself with positive people who will help you see the bright side of things.

September 25

What kinds of role models do we present to our younger siblings and the children in our care? Start shaping their future decisions right away.

My younger sister is absolutely adorable, and I adore her very much. Regardless of whether or not I was the center of attention, I was always concerned about how the decisions I made would impact the life of my younger sister. If I continue to use drugs in front of her, she will begin to accept it as normal behavior. Knowing that younger generations look up to us as role models requires us to be vigilant and cautious in everything that we do and say.

The goal is to be a good role model for the people in your life who have a significant amount of influence over you.

26 September

As long as you keep an open mind and are willing to consider other outcomes, you always have the opportunity to make the best of a challenging situation.

Every traumatic experience I've had has ultimately contributed to my growth as a person and made me into a better version of myself. I've developed both as an artist and as a person, and as a result, I'm now in a position to advocate for others who are still striving to have their voices heard. I don't know how to put into words how much of a blessing and an honor it is for me to be able to use the misery I've been through to help others find strength and, perhaps, prevent needless suffering for many more people. These rays of light were only able to penetrate the gloom because I allowed them to, because I was open to them, and because I did not dwell on my past or my grief; rather, I just appreciated them.

The objective is to derive some benefit from the difficulties currently being faced and communicate this benefit to another individual who is going through similar experiences. They will come to the realization that something better is heading their way as well.

September 27

> We are afraid to show too much concern for fear that the other person would take offense at our actions.

Never let fear prevent you from letting someone know how you feel about them. Throughout my life, there have been a lot of moments when I wanted to express how much I loved someone, but I was afraid of coming off as uncool. They gave it back to me once I got over my first disappointment and saw how appreciative they were of the loving gesture I had shown them. In order for them to be honest with me, it was necessary.

Your mission is to be truthful with at least one person in your life and to inspire others to do the same with you.

September 28

> Be punctual.

In life, it is essential to say exactly what is on your mind. Sometimes, we find ourselves hesitant to say anything that might hurt someone's feelings or let them down. On the other hand, true agony and disappointment come about when we say something that we don't mean or make a promise that we can't keep. Even I have been guilty of saying or doing things that I later came to regret, such as breaking a commitment that I knew I couldn't keep. I wished that were true, but I knew deep down that it wasn't going to be possible for me. Be sure that what you're expressing is something of which you can be proud. Even if you believe that what you are offering is not sufficiently enticing, at least you will have been honest.

The goal is to continue to take responsibility for your actions. It is important that whatever you say today is founded on honesty and the truth.

September 29

Don't postpone your enjoyment of something.

There was a time when I was experiencing a lot of melancholy. All that I ever wanted was to be happy, and I spent my entire life searching for that happiness somewhere else than within myself. Someone else's words that I overheard were, "Change your mindset, change your life." At first, I didn't believe it since I chalked up my sorrow to outside factors and other people's actions. My decision to experiment with changing the way I think led me to the discovery that I may experience happiness almost immediately. The power of the mind is incredible, and I discovered that taking responsibility for my own happiness made all the difference in the world.

The day after tomorrow may bring you happiness, but you shouldn't rely on it. Start today on the path that will lead you to happiness.

September 30

Be courageous and powerful, and support from the forces of the universe will come to you.

When you have a clear vision of what you want out of life, the only thing that matters is that you pursue that vision with conviction and fearlessness. To accomplish what you set out to do, you do not need to be completely familiar with each and every step.

The objective is to take a courageous step into the unknown while maintaining faith that the earth will appear under you at the appropriate time.

Month October, Chapter 10

October 1

> Even if there are some things in life that are beyond our control, we can still make plans for the future and choose our next steps.

Your journey through life will present you with every emotion and experience imaginable, in addition to many that you could never have conceived of. I make it a point to express gratitude for any opportunity that presents itself. The purpose of life is to live each day to the fullest, regardless of the circumstances you find yourself in.

Your objective is to think of something fantastic that is waiting for you.

October 2

> Instead of worrying, focus on being happy in the now.

Even though it's a straightforward idea, it can be quite challenging to stop worrying. Worrying over anything accomplishes nothing but puts a damper on our joy. It does what it claims to, so give it a shot and see if it lifts your spirits. Listening to music that is upbeat and enjoyable is a great way to get back on track.

October 3

> The only person who suffers when you hate is yourself, because the majority of the people you dislike are clueless and don't care what you think of them.

When I was going through a breakup, I would spend the majority of my time feeling filled with hate and loathing toward the person I had been with. Although I didn't realize it at the time, I was exposed to a great deal of toxicity throughout my life. I used to wonder why my exes managed to get over their breakups and move on with their lives so much more quickly than I did. I now see that the reason behind this was that I focused so much of my energy on being angry with them rather than moving on with my life. I spent more time being angry at my bullies when I was twelve years old than I did loving and caring for myself.

Aim: Regardless of the challenges you face in life, you should make it a point to avoid self-harming behaviors like harboring resentment rather than practicing self-love.

4 October

> An open heart is the single most significant quality that a person may possess.

It's impossible to predict when or how something lovely will show up in your life. You might have your mind made up on one thing, but the universe actually has something far more wonderful in store for you. If you only look in one direction, you might not notice it. It is essential to keep your attention on your goals and objectives even as you have an open mind about potential outcomes.

The goal for today is to challenge yourself by doing something that you normally wouldn't do and observing how it makes you feel. You might get a fresh appreciation for an element of your life.

5 October

> Although we cannot start over, we can start anew right now and come up with a new conclusion.

Permit the goals, ambitions, and visions for your life to fill your heart, revitalize and influence every word that you utter, and bring new meaning to each step that you take.

You should make it a goal to be fearless, ambitious, bold, and courageous in both your personal and professional lives.

October 6

The things that are most magnificent are the ones that are the simplest, but only those who are knowledgeable can notice them.

When was the last time you stopped to take a moment to notice the world around you? There are a lot of simple things to notice in this life. Be careful not to become so immersed in your own world that you lose sight of everything else going on around you.

The objective is to take in as many fragments and moments as you possibly can.

The seventh of October

Individuals who are very proud bring bad luck upon themselves.

I think that a lot of us have been too proud to ask for help or to confess that we didn't know something, and that's unfortunate. It's possible that our pride is getting in the way of our ability to learn new things. Never be hesitant to ask for help or to admit that you do not fully understand something; never be scared to do either of these things.

In the event that you are unsure of something, make sure to ask plenty of questions. You are not weak; you are just learning more and getting a broader view of things.

October 8

If a promise is not honored right away, it will lose its luster over time, just like the full moon.

It's simple enough for us to say that we'll act, but if we don't actually do it, our words will be nothing more than empty promises. If you are unable to follow through on your commitments, especially those to yourself, you will not only cause harm to others, but you will also jeopardize your own integrity.

A sincere apology should be offered to everyone who you may have wronged in the recent past by breaking a promise or commitment made to them.

Day 9 of October

There is only one way to avoid being criticized, and that is to not speak, act, or do anything at all.

You are not expected to please everyone, nor are you able to, and that is okay. I have been the recipient of a great deal of criticism, and I have even seen some unpleasant remarks posted on the internet; however, I am not going to allow any of it to get to me. All I need to do is maintain my authenticity in the presence of the people who are truly important to me, and that will be sufficient.

The objective is to focus on rewarding yourself rather than making it your mission to please others. Don't respond to someone who is continually critical of you if you can help it.

The tenth of October

Ego is a social fiction in which one person is fully responsible for their actions.

We are not our egos, and so we cannot blame them for everything that goes wrong in our lives. We have no choice but to take responsibility for the decisions we make in life, even if this requires us to go against our own feelings in order to achieve the goals we have set for ourselves, despite the fact that it is challenging for our pride.

The objective is to let go of your ego and take responsibility for the things you do.

The eleventh of October

> Respond intelligently even when dealing with those who are uneducated.

There are people in your life who will try to bring you down to their level with the things they say. However, every one of us has a choice in how we react when faced with such abuse. When all you want to do is make the other person feel as terrible as they've made you feel, it can be tough to keep quiet about how you really feel. However, let me reassure you that doing so is never the answer. Be patient and gracious in your response, not for the benefit of the other person but rather for the good of yourself.

When someone treats you poorly in the future, the goal is to not react in the same manner. Be the more mature person in how you respond to this situation.

12th of October

> Inevitably, life will present you with adversity and unpredictability. But you have to treat them with respect because they have skills too.

A significant amount of good has come to me as a result of all of the challenges I've faced and the road I've taken. They have been essential to my growth, not only as an artist but also as a person. After acknowledging the difficulties, I was facing and deciding to grow as a result of those difficulties rather than letting them dictate my actions, I started to feel a lot better. Now that I look back on it, I can see how the challenges and troubles I faced helped me grow as an artist and as a woman.

When you're surrounded by chaos, it's important to remember that many positive things will happen in response to it.

The 13th of October

> Keep your distance from people who laugh at your ambitions. This is something that people of a lower social standing always do, but those who are truly great inspire you to feel that you, too, are capable of achieving greatness.

The easiest method for me to determine whether someone is a true friend or not is to consider whether they want to help me improve myself or whether they want to bring me down. I only want to spend my time with other people who lift me up and make me feel more powerful thanks to the love and faith they have in me, as well as the love and faith I have in them. It is impossible to create a friendship that only benefits one person; both parties must benefit from the relationship.

The end goal is to determine whether or not it is beneficial to communicate your feelings to a toxic person in your life. If they are unwilling to change the way they act toward you, you should try limiting the amount of time you spend with them.

The 14th of October

> The biggest jump was made by a wounded deer.

The wounds and scars we've endured have made us stronger and more courageous. Because of this, each passing moment of my life has taken on greater significance, and as a direct result, I am more familiar with myself. I've become more resilient, and my appreciation for life has also grown. I'm now in a place where I can thank my injuries for the good things they've done for me.

Accepting your past hardships and problems is the goal of this project because they helped shape who you are now. You have become more resilient as a result of all that has happened to you, and despite everything, you are here today to talk about it.

October 15

> There was not a single day in which God was able to complete everything. What leads you to believe that you are capable of doing so?

No matter how strenuous your task is, it is imperative that you take breaks at regular intervals. Get up off the ground, stretch your muscles, and then do a five-minute meditation to bring some peace to your mind. When you go back to your job, you will find that you are more productive than before. Because I enjoy what I do so much, it is not difficult for me to lose myself in my work, even when I am in the studio for sixteen hours straight. It is absolutely necessary for me to get up and get some air outside. My disposition is enhanced, and the challenge of my work is maintained thanks to it.

Your mission is to revitalize yourself by giving yourself some time each day to focus on you.

The 16th of October

> Words have the power to both hurt and help those who hear them. Words have the ability to change the world when they are said in a way that is both sincere and kind.

Our words have far more power than we give them credit for. They are capable of causing both good and evil in their environment. They have the ability to either bring people together or instigate violence among them. It is easy for us to lash out at people when we are suffering the most pain; yet, in doing so, we are contributing to the struggle that we are now going through. If you take your frustration out on other people, you will only end up making the same mistakes over and over again.

The goal is to locate as many healthy outlets as possible if you are experiencing discomfort. Find a friend to talk to, express yourself creatively, keep a journal, or seek the advice of a qualified expert.

October 17.

> The most significant thing we can do to contribute to the overall healing of the earth currently is to forgive those who have wronged us.

Everyone in the world would be filled with resentment, bitterness, and would be stuck in the present if everyone continued to concentrate on past wrongs and suffering. Because of this, there would be no hope for the future. The act of exhibiting humility in a contagious way shows that you can set aside your ego and come to the realization that it is more essential to be happy and at peace than to be "correct." The act of forgiving others has a transformational effect that goes beyond words.

Taking everything into consideration, it might be best for you to forgive!

Instead of wasting time worrying about whether what you are doing is appropriate, the objective is to focus your energy on pursuits that make you happy.

The 18th of October

> Never, ever quit.

This is a sentence that everyone of us has undoubtedly been exposed to a great deal throughout our lives. It wasn't until I started living by this philosophy that I realized why so many cliched remarks are actually accurate. When your hopes and beliefs are put to the test, it does not necessarily follow that there is no more room for optimism.

Instead, it suggests that someone is evaluating you for something. Your supplications will be heard, and your goals and desires will come to fruition when you rise above the challenges that you are facing and show the universe that you want what you want in spite of everything.

Consider what it is in life that brings you the most joy, and make it a priority to do more of that.

The 19th of October

People frequently argue that motivation is not something that can be sustained. On the other hand, taking a shower does not, which is why we recommend that you do it on a daily basis.

Keep in mind that regardless of the goals you now have, you need to make daily progress toward achieving them. It is not enough to simply write down your future goals and ambitions; in order to accomplish anything in life, you will need to put in a lot of effort.

Aim: During this month, make it a priority to carry out at least one task each day that will bring you one step closer to achieving your objective.

20 October

If we wait until everything, including the kitchen sink, is ready before we start, we will never get anything done.

Don't sit around idly waiting for the right opportunity to act. There is no such thing as a suitable moment to do anything. If I had waited until the most opportune moment to launch my career, I probably would not be where I am right now. Put in the work, and don't limit your ambitions. You only need to get out there and make things happen for yourself to complete this task.

Put an end to putting off working on a goal you have.

The 21st of October

If the knowledge gained from an event is applied appropriately, then none of that time was ever wasted.

Finding out who I am has taken up a significant portion of both my journey and my life. When I was younger, I had the misconception that if I didn't already know something, there was no way I could ever learn it. Now I realize that the journey and the process, together, defined and completed me as a person. Taking risks, expanding one's horizons, and remaining open to new experiences are the most important things to focus on. I am aware that I am being guided there, and that is the only thing that matters. I would like to keep growing, gaining knowledge, and uncovering new things. Embrace the mystery, for it is there that you will find all of the magic.

The goal is to be grateful for your journey because it is something that only you have experienced.

The 22nd of October

When it comes to love, we always challenge ourselves to be better than we already are. Everything in our environment gets better when we strive to be better than we already are.

Love is the most powerful agent of healing, and it is also the best medication. Love is the force that makes everything possible. It not only empowers us but also enables us to be more open and kinder than we could have ever imagined being before we received this gift. There is no such thing as having too much love in your heart. People will admire your capacity to love completely and completely from the bottom of their hearts.

The end goal is to heal yourself through the love of others and the love you feel for yourself.

The 23rd of October

Therefore, I'm going to start my escape from this jail today. I've decided to get out of bed and face my demons.

No matter what you have been through in life, there is always a chance for you to break free and prevail over the challenges you have faced. Before many of us can pass beyond this threshold, we must first endure something truly horrible. Remember that things will get better and that you always have the option to get treatment and face your demons, no matter what the circumstances of your current scenario may be.

Look deep within yourself, amass all of your strength, and confront whatever it is that is holding you back. That is the goal.

The 24th of October

When you look back on the past twenty years, you will be more dissatisfied by the things you did not accomplish than by the things you did.

Therefore, release your grip on the bowlines. Leave the safety of the secure harbor and set sail. Take advantage of the favorable trade winds that are blowing in your direction. Explore. Dream. Explore. As an artist, you have to have the courage to pursue the goals you set for yourself. You have to be willing to step outside of your comfort zone in order to grow as a person and test the boundaries of your own abilities. I encourage everyone who is working toward achieving a goal to have courage and to explore areas of their emotions that aren't always straightforward or easily understood.

The mission for the day is to engage in an activity that is outside of your usual routine. Things that make us anxious can, on occasion, be beneficial to our growth.

October 25th

Never assume anything, never inquire, never demand, and never anticipate anything. Let it be as it is. Because everything that is intended to be will eventually come to pass.

When we accept that the only thing we have control over in this life are our own actions, it can feel limiting and even awkward because we all crave complete control over some aspect of our lives. But the more

I thought about it, the more I realized how little I actually knew about it, and that realization set me free. There is a possibility that not everything will go according to plan, but in the end, everything will turn out as it should.

Think about a part of your life that you don't currently have control over and try to find peace in that area.

The 26th of October

Your self-righteousness will increase along with your rage, so be aware of it and try to look at it from as many different perspectives as possible.

Because anger is such a powerful emotion, when it takes hold of us, it tends to cloud our judgment and interfere with our ability to think clearly. We have to be honest about how we feel while also being aware that letting our anger get the best of us could make it hard for us to think clearly.

You must control your anger and not let it get the better of you. Think about how your feelings can be explained logically, and be aware of the impact they have on other people.

October 27

We won't be able to change the world unless we first change ourselves.

As flawed humans living on this earth, it is essential that we retain an open mind, continue growing, and expand our horizons. When we work to better ourselves and our lives, we contribute to making the world a better place for everyone else.

The objective is to get involved in some kind of philanthropic work and to make the world a better place.

The 28th of October

> It is impossible to live your life for the benefit of other people. You have no choice but to act in a manner that puts you first, even if it means offending the people who are important to you.

Celebrate your independence and the opportunity to choose how you want to live your life today. It might be challenging to win over the approval of those around you, but you should always strive to make the choices that are in your own best interests. In the final analysis, that is the only thing you need to be concerned about.

The goal is to avoid basing your decisions on the thoughts and recommendations of other people.

The 29th of October

> In spite of everything, I still have the impression that people are, at their core, good.

If Anne Frank, who lived through horrific tragedies, was able to keep a positive outlook and have faith in the goodwill of people, then I have no excuse not to do the same.

When you're feeling sorry for yourself or in need of some perspective, your goal should be to remind yourself of how incredible your life is. You are fortunate.

October 30

> If you turn your back to the light and keep your face toward it, you won't be able to see any shadows.

It's incredible to think that someone who couldn't even see could come up with such an observation. Simply by shifting her perspective, she was able to perceive the light that resides inside herself as well as within each of us; this is a great attitude from which we can all take something to improve ourselves.

Aim: If you make the conscious decision to surround yourself with positive people, you will be able to effectively deal with any challenges that come your way.

October 31st

One of the most terrifying things that can happen in life is realizing that the only person or thing that can save you is... yourself.

After going to counseling, I came to the realization that no one could save me unless I took responsibility for my own well-being, regardless of how many people I counted on for support. The only way to bring about change is from within, not from elsewhere. You can't coerce someone into making a change.

The goal of this exercise is to do a self-evaluation and provide an open and honest response to the question, "Do I need guidance?"

Month November, Chapter 11

November 1

> How did it get to be so late so quickly? Before noon, there is complete darkness. The month of December will come before June. How fast time has flown by over the years! How did it get to be such a late hour so suddenly?

The speed with which time moves through our lives continues to astonish and amaze me. As I get older, it feels like everything is moving quicker and faster. When you're a kid, a day can feel like it goes on and on for an eternity. It is a good reminder that we should value each and every moment in our lives, regardless of how big or small it may be, as well as each and every person who comes into our lives.

Your goal should be to not let another day go by without accomplishing something meaningful, either for yourself or for other people.

November 2

> There is only one page left for you to complete. I'll pack it full of words that only have one syllable. I adore. It was fantastic. It's going to be wonderful for me.

It is not necessary to be a 10-year-old girl in order to keep a life journal or notebook. It is quite important to keep a journal in which you record everything that occurs in your life as well as how you feel about it. Not only can it help you get a better understanding of what's going on around you, but it's also a wonderful thing to look back on as you get older. When something good happens in our lives, we always think we will remember it, but the truth is that if we don't write it down, we won't. Consider how valuable it will be for you in the future to read about your life and the things you did.

Your mission is to document your life and your feelings in a journal, notebook, or other space that is completely dedicated to you.

November 3

> You will never know how strong you are until you are put in a position where you have no choice but to be strong.

When we are confronted with difficulties in life, we have the opportunity to demonstrate that we are equal to the task at hand. When you do this, you better prepare yourself to face the situation at hand and develop a character that is as strong as it is possible for you to be.

When faced with challenging circumstances, it is important to remember not to underrate your own capabilities. Be proud of your fortitude.

November 4

> Everything that comes to my mind has the ability to make me different. But I refuse to allow myself to be brought down by it.

Each activity that we participate in is organized to teach us something new, put us in our place, and advance our growth. Nobody or anything on this earth should ever have the power to make us feel less than we are. You can't avoid being changed by life, but you don't have to let it bring you down. If someone ever makes you feel less than because they believe you are growing or learning, it is only a reflection of their own dissatisfaction.

The goal here is to not let anyone else tell you how you should be feeling.

November 5

> It is said that the eyes are the windows to the soul.

When people talk to one another without looking the other person in the eyes while they do it, it is one of my biggest pet peeves. When we talk from the heart, each of us carries a great deal of power; yet, if we communicate without genuinely looking at the other person, we won't be able to form meaningful connections with them.

It is often through a person's eyes rather than their words that we are able to get a sense of how they are truly feeling. Body language conveys a great deal of information, so be aware of how you carry yourself at all times.

When you talk to someone, make it a point to look them in the eye and establish a connection with them. They will have greater regard for you, and you will have more respect for yourself as a result of their increased regard.

November 6

> If you are now experiencing hell, keep moving forward.

Don't view other people's bad days as a reflection on you; everyone goes through rough patches. Even if we had access to all of the information and advice in the world, we would still experience difficult times. It is not your responsibility if another person is having a bad day and is irritable toward you because of it.

Give them some time to cool off. There are days like that for all of us. Get some sleep and unwind for a while. It won't last forever. If you're having a bad day, unplug your devices and try to relax. November 7 is National Take Time for Yourself Day.

I don't pretend to be perfect, nor do I feel the need to.

The realization that this was the case brought me a great deal of peace. This realization helped me develop into a more well-rounded individual. It instilled in me the confidence to acknowledge my shortcomings and to grow as a result of my mistakes.

The pressure gradually decreased. If I had been under the impression that I needed to be perfect, I would not have been able to begin working on improving the areas in which I fall short. After I came to terms with the fact that it was okay to have shortcomings, everything began to improve.

Instead of berating oneself for making mistakes, the goal is to work on avoiding repeating the same blunder over and over again.

November 8

Self-portraiture is something I do since I spend a lot of time by myself and because I am the person with whom I have the most experience.

All we can do is be faithful to ourselves and honor those aspects of ourselves that are most essential and authentic. Music has been the one and only thing that has ever provided me with complete solace on a number of occasions throughout my life.

It was quite encouraging to me to realize that I could sit in my room by myself and compose a song that accurately conveyed how I felt. It instilled in me an appreciation for the solitude I like. I really want every one of you to find something similar and keep working on it every day.

The goal is to make the things that you care about most your strongest allies and protectors.

November 9

> Now I am a warrior, with thicker skin and stronger muscles than I've ever had, and my armor is made of steel. You can't get in; I'm a warrior, and you can never harm me again. I've become stronger than I've ever been.

When I was writing these words, I had something specific in mind, but anyone who has ever been forced to go through anything terrible can relate to the sentiments expressed in them. Because I talk to a lot of people who have been through a variety of traumatic experiences in their lives but are unable to speak up for themselves because of embarrassment or fear, this song and the message it conveys are of the utmost significance to me.

I wrote this song to serve as a gentle yet powerful reminder to people of all ages that they are never truly alone and that there is always assistance available to them.

November 10

> Be aware of the fact that while it can be challenging to make things straightforward, it is really simple to make them convoluted.

It comes naturally to us to overthink and make everything more complicated than it has to be. Our lives are usually difficult, and many of the challenges we face appear insurmountable. They argue that the solution that is the simplest is almost always the correct one, so when I'm feeling overwhelmed, I try to remember the core notion of simplicity. When in doubt, try clearing your mind of as much mental clutter as possible.

Think of your problem as a knot that you need to untie. Your task is to untie that knot.

November 11

Judging a person is not the same as defining them. It has a significant impact on who you are.

I've been through a lot, and I've done a lot of things that are grounds for criticism, so I'm used to hearing it. It is not my place to judge the path taken by another individual, and I would never point the finger of blame at another person for the decisions they make. It is also none of anyone's business to comment on the quality of my work.

The goal is to refrain from passing judgment on other people. Think about the way you'd like to be treated and act accordingly.

November 12

In this place, there are no unknown people—simply friends waiting to be made.

The great advances that have been made in social media have created a society that is becoming more interconnected on a daily basis. It is great to wake up to good remarks from my followers located all over the world on social media platforms like Twitter and Facebook, and it is even more incredible to realize that I have friends and fans no matter where I go.

The astonishing thing is that this is true for each and every one of us. When we begin to see the world as a welcoming environment that nourishes and supports us, the universe opens up to us. Once we realize that the possibilities are virtually endless, we are able to access the infinite potential that lies within it.

The goal for today is to stay open to meeting new people and making new friends.

November 13

> If things were easy to find, there would be no use in searching for them in the first place.

I count it as a blessing that, from a very young age, I had a clear vision of the things I wanted to achieve during my lifetime. On the other hand, I know a lot of people who are still grappling with the question of what exactly it means for them. You will find that place within yourself if you keep an open mind and continue to pursue your goals, even if they appear to be underdeveloped at the moment. Doing something that you've always wanted to do is the objective of this game. In the event that you are not already doing so, there is no better moment than the present to start.

November 14

> Forgiveness is the single most irritating thing you can do to your enemies.

Forgiveness can be challenging, especially in situations where you feel you have been severely wronged by another person. However, you demonstrate that you are a more mature and compassionate person whenever you forgive another individual. It is unhealthy to focus on the wrongs done to you by another person since it is likely that they have already forgiven themselves for their transgressions by the time you get around to thinking about them.

They should be mercilessly put to death. When you forgive another individual, you demonstrate that you are a more mature and compassionate person. When I was a child and was being bullied, my mother always reminded me to show the other person the cheek. When I was of an age where I could properly comprehend the idiom, I was able to put it into practice. In addition to that, it helped me get over my hostility toward the person.

The objective here is to let go of your resentment and forgive the person who has caused you annoyance.

November 15

> The fruit of one's patience may be bitter, but the difficulty of obtaining it is more than worth it.

Having patience in life can be challenging, especially when dealing with other people or when desiring something very much yet having to wait for it for a significant amount of time. People can have to wait years or even decades before they achieve what they've been working toward. This is something that's possible. Have faith that things will come to you at the right time, and be aware that the benefits will exceed everything you could possibly have hoped for as a result of your efforts.

Be patient not only with the people around you but also with your goals and, most importantly, with yourself. This is the goal.

November 16

> Violence produces more violence. Everyone here should try to be a soldier of peace.

The cycle of violence never comes to an end. It is far easier to fight fire with fire, yet this is an undertaking that cannot possibly succeed. It takes a lot more effort, thinking, inventiveness, and bravery to get up and participate in a debate with someone who disagrees with you than it does to engage in a conversation with someone who agrees with you. You can still show respect and tolerance even if you don't agree with someone. Even when we have different opinions, we should still be willing to communicate with one another and respect one another.

The objective is to fight against violence while simultaneously demanding respect and open dialogue. Keep an open mind and try to see things from many angles. Keep an open mind and try to see things from the other person's perspective.

November 17

> Instead of being punished because of your rage, you will receive it as a result of it.

Anger and resentment are two of the most potentially harmful feelings that we are capable of experiencing. There are times when someone aggravates us or hurts our feelings, but we choose not to address them despite the fact that we should. Instead, we give these bad emotions free reign within us and let them consume us. Before we are even aware of it, they have wriggled their way through every cell and organ in our bodies, taking over like vines. We should never let the problems of others bring us down in the first place, and we should never allow it to happen.

Don't hold a grudge against someone who has offended you; instead, talk to them about it and then do everything you can to put the matter behind you.

November 18

> Please take my hand in yours, and together we will figure this out.

Your thoughts and ideals alone are not enough to make a relationship work since it takes two people to have a healthy and successful connection. You must make it possible for the other person to communicate their thoughts and feelings. It does not imply that you are required to agree on everything; in fact, you will not, and there is nothing wrong with that. On the other hand, you will be on your own if you are unable to reach a compromise or a middle ground. When you run into a problem, it's best to pool the resources of your friends, family, and coworkers to figure out a solution.

November 19

> Make the most of what you have and the situation you're in by giving it your all.

Everyone has the right to be treated with respect and to be aware of their place in the hierarchy. On the other hand, a lot of the girlfriends I know put up with their partners' poor treatment of them. These individuals deceive others about their genuine intentions and make false promises that they are unable to keep. When my friend had been dating a man for about a month, she informed him that she truly loved him and wanted a partner, not just a casual hookup. She wanted a committed relationship.

However, he never made a commitment to her because he kept the lines of their relationship so blurry. She was adamant that if the two of them spent additional time together, she would be able to change him and convince him to love her. Naturally, she did not in any way change him. He wasted no time in exposing his true nature, but she ignored the red flags he raised because she had higher hopes for him. Do not persist with someone who refuses to commit to anything or who is unable to do so for any reason. Accept it or leave.

November 20

> Give God the reins of your life.

When all else fails and you're fighting against something bigger than yourself, you simply need to be ready to hand over your problems to somebody who is more powerful than you are. Regardless of whether you believe in God, Allah, or the power of the cosmos, each of us is encircled by a force that is more powerful than ourselves. Realizing and accepting that you don't have full control over your life is actually very freeing and can have big effects.

Think about the things you're clinging to, take a few slow, deep breaths, and then hand them over to the force that is larger than you.

November 21

> You are the one who holds the key to your pleasure; your phone is not the source of it.

We all spend so much time on our phones that they are practically inseparable from us at this point. I don't pass judgment because I frequently run into the same problem, but as of late, I've been trying to fight the urge to go for my phone. I recently came to the realization that I was using it as a distraction in order to avoid my thoughts, but in actuality I needed to be embracing them.

The task for the day is to refrain from using your phone. Take a few deep breaths and look around you for anything or someone nice to enjoy whenever you get the desire to engage in mindless activities such as playing games, looking at pictures, or reading old text messages.

November 22

> In the same way that using a credit card can be fun up until the time that payment is due, so can procrastination.

Even though everyone is aware that they should not postpone, most of us nonetheless do so on occasion. You will experience a feeling of being out of control as well as agitation if you continue to put things off since they will continue to pile up.

The goal is to organize your responsibilities and time according to your priorities.

November 23

> There is no room for faith where there is complete assurance.

This was said by my pastor during one of his sermons, and I was profoundly moved by both the content of the statement and the way the sentence was constructed. There are times when each and every one of us questions why we are here and if we are acting in an appropriate manner. It is healthy and appropriate to question your direction in life because doing so demonstrates that you care and are present in the moment. If you never had any questions or concerns, there would be nothing worth putting your faith in.

The goal is to acknowledge that you are worried and to think about why you are worried.

November 24

> If you think in a plentiful manner, you will be rewarded in a plentiful manner.

You should allow yourself to consider everything you want your life to be. If something enters your mind and you immediately think it's too much or that you can't have it, push those thoughts out of your head as quickly as they came in. Create a list of all the goals, resolutions, and expectations you have for the upcoming year.

November 25

> Strength and the development of our characters come to us from our families.

Without the unconditional love, unwavering faith, and unwavering support of my family, none of what I have accomplished would have been possible. Simply being in the same room as them makes me feel content and helps me forget about the concerns and worries I have. They accept me despite the fact that I am full of flaws, and I do the same for them.

The love and support of your family should be the focus of today's activities. Love them despite the fact that they are not who you want them to be.

November 26

> It doesn't matter how slowly you move as long as you don't stop at any of the checkpoints.

The concept of speed is relative. There are those that go quickly, while others like to take their time. It is not important how much work you get done; what is important is that you keep moving forward regardless of the outcome. no matter what the circumstances are.

The objective for today is to take it easy throughout the whole day, from the moment you open your eyes to the time you close them and everything in between.

November 27

> Do your best to keep your composure.

In this life, something bad happens to each and every one of us. I came to the realization that no matter where I am, I serve a greater purpose by using my voice to inspire others, to help people work through difficulties, and to aid people in getting back up on their feet when they are down. It is only because of my followers that I am able to make it through each day. They always motivate me to keep doing what I do and to be strong.

Find the strength to continue being strong for yourself, and if you have it in you, find the strength to continue being strong for someone else as well. This is your goal.

November 28

> When your problems are bigger than you can handle on your own, it is imperative that you seek support.

Because of our challenges, we could experience feelings of helplessness and even embarrassment at times. Before I started going to therapy for my bulimia and cutting, I had resorted to concealing everything from everyone, including myself. I was too embarrassed to ask for help, and I was so ashamed of what I was doing that I believed I would never be able to stop doing it. I was unable to seek assistance because of my fear. If you or someone you care about is hurting or struggling with any kind of problem, it is critical to get professional treatment. You could end up saving not just your own life but also the life of another person.

The objective is to not hide anything from yourself or other people. Try to get help.

November 29

> One advantage of rain is that it never lasts forever; eventually it stops falling. Eventually.

Difficulties are unavoidable. They show up when we least expect it, which is precisely when we are not ready for them. However, it is essential to keep in mind that this cannot and will not continue on indefinitely.

The goal is to keep reminding yourself that the difficulties you are experiencing are just serving to fortify your character as you move forward.

November 30

> When you lose your chuckle, you lose your balance.

There will be times when we feel as though we are being brought to our knees at every turn. These periods are inevitable. There is grief, despair, broken relationships, and a whole host of other problems. It is essential to maintain a healthy sense of humor.

You have to make a point of laughing at these things, or else you'll let them take control of you. Even in the most hopeless of circumstances, laughter may help you find the silver lining. It has a stronger impact than you probably know.

The objective is to keep and make use of your sense of humor, even when you are feeling at your worst.

Month December, Chapter 12

December 1

> We bid farewell to the old year and welcome the new, which brings with it many things that have never existed before.

Spend some time doing some introspection about the past year. Think about the ways in which you've developed and changed, as well as the things you'd like to keep doing and the things you're ready to give up. The last few days of the year always feel to me like they are packed with so much powerful energy and possibility for change that the best thing you can do during that time is just sit and think about things.

December 2

> You are the only person who will advocate on your behalf; no one else will.

There have been times in my life when I have been in situations where I recognized that the way I was being treated was inappropriate, but I was unable to speak out for myself due to fear or shyness. Due to the fact that I believe most of us have an irrational fear of being disliked, this might be rather challenging and terrifying for people.

On the other hand, if you do not stand up for what you believe in, others will take advantage of you. It makes no difference whether it was done on purpose or by accident; the result is the same. My opinion is that you will get a lot more respect if you start speaking up for yourself.

Take charge of your life by learning to stand up for yourself in smart, sure ways.

On December 3,

> Remember to love who you are and accept who you were born to be.

It is possible that being bullied or taunted will have long-term repercussions for the victim. When I was younger, I was making changes to aspects of myself that bullies didn't like, and as a result, I was beginning to lose my identity. I woke up one day with the realization that I was no longer the same person. It was necessary for me to acknowledge and accept myself exactly as I am and have always been. After learning this, I was able to have a more positive attitude toward myself.

The objective is to never change who you are in order to live up to the standards set by other people.

December 4

> Show kindness to those who are cruel, since they are the ones who need it most.

When you start paying attention to random people, you will notice that some people give off the impression that they are genuinely happy, while others look to be angry at the state of the world. Remember that those people are probably going through a lot on the inside, so try not to take it personally. Think about the gloomy person standing next to you in line or the security officer at the airport who is yelling at everyone; such people are clearly acting out because they are going through something dreadful on the inside. They are in dire need of compassion, and they will be profoundly impacted by your gesture, even if you are unable to convey the sympathy that you feel for them. If you show them that you are weak in front of them, it is quite likely that they will do the same in front of you.

The mission for the day is to respond constructively to anger.

December 5

> It's a good sign to have a broken heart since it shows that we gave it our all and attempted to achieve something.

There will always be times when we put in a lot of effort for something, only to be disappointed in our efforts. It demonstrates that you are open to trying new things and taking risks. I really hope that despite the fact that the pain is awful, you can keep in mind that it is a good sign that you care. It reflects all the love that is contained within you.

The objective is to love with all of your heart in a way that is fearless and brave.

December 6

> There is no one who is deserving of your tears, and even those who are will not make you cry for them.

There are going to be a lot of people in your life who will either bring tears to your eyes or make you feel like crying. Those people have nothing to do with your sadness and do not deserve it. People who are able to comfort you and assist you in wiping away your tears are the same people who would never cause you to feel in such a manner. Your goal should be to surround yourself with individuals who, when things are bad, will be there to console and encourage you.

December 7

> We should feel regret for our mistakes and grow as a result of them, but we should never let those mistakes define us moving forward.

Even if we are well aware that none of us is perfect, this fact does not prevent us from engaging in behaviors that we will come to deeply regret in the future. In predicaments such as this one, I've learned that it's preferable to come clean and accept responsibility for whatever transpired. If you are straightforward and sincere about it, people will have far more compassion and forgiveness for you. Even better, if you show others that you can be honest and attractive even when you have flaws, they will be inspired to act like you and try to be perfect themselves.

Today's mission is to reflect on anything you've done or said in the past 30 days that you wish you could take back.

December 8

> When was the last time you gave your true self an honest appraisal?

In life, it is necessary for us to frequently take stock of where we are and how we are feeling. The very first time I heard this statement, the first thing that went through my head was, "Wow, am I being myself right now, or am I merely trying to fit in with whatever it is that society wants me to be?" It is important to always keep in mind that you should be true to yourself, and it is a good idea to remind yourself of this.

Finding oneself while being true to one's core values should be the objective here.

December 9

> I often dream that I am painting, and when I wake up, I paint what I saw in my sleep.

Your dreams are great gifts that you have been given. My entire life, I've had the dream of being on stage. I aspired to have talent in singing, dancing, and acting. These goals made it possible for me to pursue the things that I wanted. I am thankful that I was able to achieve my goals and arrive at this point in my life. Put in a lot of effort to make your goals and dreams a reality. Your goals and aspirations can only be accomplished by you.

December 10

> It's important for everyone to have someone they can look up to.

Where I am at this very moment... There are still highs and lows in my life, but I try to take each day as it comes. Simply put, I just want to be the best possible version of myself, not only for my own sake but also for the sake of others around me. Everyone has a need for constructive influences in their lives, and it is essential that we surround ourselves with people who can provide those influences.

Who do you look up to? When you go out of your way to help other people, you increase the likelihood that you will be seen as a positive influence and an example to others.

December 11

> Recognize that the best thing you can do is to focus on the here and now in accordance with your current desires.

We have no choice except to simply take each day and each moment as they come. It will only serve to direct you in the wrong direction if you allow yourself to become overly preoccupied with our past or our future. Because the present is all that we have, it is essential to establish a strong foundation for yourself in the moment that you are currently living in so that you can recognize your presence in this world.

Take your mind off of both the past and the future for a moment. Focus your attention solely on the here and now.

December 12

> When you decide to enjoy the journey, the destination is no longer a condition for your happiness.

Even if you have your hopes set on a particular outcome, you shouldn't let stress get the better of you. We never get exactly what we expect or hope for because the results are very different and unpredictable.

Appreciate and treasure the process, and have faith that everything else will fall into place at the exact time it is supposed to. Consider a time when the journey to achieving a goal was more satisfying than the accomplishment of the goal itself.

December 13

> No matter what you do for a living or what your interests are, you need to have self-control.

It is not enough to simply enjoy doing something in order to excel at it. You must also put in the necessary work. You are required to engage in practice every day. Before I can do a performance, head out on tour, or record in the studio, I have to perfect my singing and playing of my songs. If I simply show up on the day without any preparation, I won't be able to live up to the lofty expectations I've set for myself.

Make room in your calendar so that you can pursue the things that interest you. Do whatever it takes to move you closer to achieving the goals you've set for yourself.

December 14

> When you get to the end of your rope, tie a knot in it and hang on for dear life.

When it seems as though there is nothing you can do, keep holding on. At some point, something else will show up to give you another choice, and by that time, you will have already decided what to do. Never, ever give up or let go.

The objective is to have faith in the future, even if you are unsure of what it may bring.

December 15

> Follow the dictates of your internal compass.

Your behaviors are directed by an emotion or voice that comes from deep within you and is known as your conscience. Over the course of our lives, we have gained a significant amount of knowledge from our parents, teachers, friends, and coworkers. In the end, we can only rely on the lessons we've learned and the guidance our intuition provides to determine what's best for us.

Making apologies for any wrongdoing, no matter how small, should be the goal in order to clear your mind and conscience.

December 16

> Playing games makes life more fun.

I believe that the reason we were placed on this earth is, above all else, to learn to value the time that we have. Because one's time on earth is limited, one should not allow trivial concerns to cause undue stress or strain. Take in the experience and allow yourself to feel pleasure, in whatever form that takes for you. The objective is to enjoy one's free time socializing with one's family and friends. Have a good time and make some memories for yourself.

December 17

> The word "no" is considered to be a complete sentence.

Simply responding with "no" is all that is required because no one else in this world can comprehend the boundaries you set for yourself. If anything doesn't make sense or appears out of place, pay attention to that voice. It is sufficient to respond with either yes or no; there is no requirement for you to explain yourself further. The people you spend the most time with ought to have that comprehension.

The objective is to get over the fear of declining an offer. You are in no way obligated to offer any answer or response that you do not voluntarily provide to the question.

December 18

> It's not always the case that those who wander end up lost.

If you stay on your current course, you will eventually arrive at the destination that you have always intended to visit. You never reached a point when you were lost, regardless of whether the destination you sought was a dead end or a light at the end of the tunnel. Your journey was meant to teach you something, and that is all you were intended to take away from it.

Don't stress if you can't see where you're going right now, since that's not a problem. It merely indicates that you are approaching your trip in a different manner and does not signify that you are roaming aimlessly.

December 19

> Girls will act as if they are your friends, or will give the impression that they are.

However, keep in mind that some people enter while others leave. True friends are individuals who are there for you no matter what circumstances you find yourself in. They shouldn't be allowed to go. There is a possibility that girls will be quite judgmental of one another. The nasty and upsetting behavior of the girls toward me was triggered by their taunting. I've learned what to look for in a relationship as well as how to recognize when it's time to end it. When I'm feeling sad, having a difficult day, or in need of a shoulder to cry on, my closest friends are the first ones to come to my aid.

Create a list of the ladies who are most important to you and get in touch with each one to tell them how much you value their friendship, support, and love.

December 20

> Be thankful for what you already have since you will likely obtain even more in the future. If you concentrate on the things that you do not have, you will never have enough of those things.

When we make the conscious decision to focus on what we already possess, we experience immediate happiness. Many people believe that gratitude is the emotion that is most intrinsically linked to contentment. Even the wealthiest people in the world occasionally daydream about possessions they just do not have. It is not about accumulating more things; rather, it is about focusing on the pleasure and beauty that are already there in your life by paying attention to the things that make it so amazing.

Aim: Don't base your happiness on the material possessions you have, but rather on the relationships you have in your life right now.

December 21

> The most formidable obstacle to straightforward communication is dishonesty.

Observing people who are dishonest with other people is one of the things that irritates me the most. People are always able to detect when someone is not being honest, and if you are not genuine with yourself, you are only fooling yourself into believing something that is not the case.

Talk must be kept solemn and polite at all times.

December 22

> What is meant by the term "spiritual discovery" is the realization that all that I see, experience, believe, or feel is not ultimately who I am and that I cannot find myself in everything that is constantly changing.

On the road to one's spiritual awakening, this is a very significant step to take.

Those things that we are unable to fully describe or comprehend are the ones that hold the most significant amount of truth and significance. Being unable to convey the significance of something in a clear and concise manner is both humbling and invaluable. It is not always necessary to find the ideal words to explain what is going through one's head.

Gratitude for the experiences that have allowed one to feel things that they aren't always able to express, together with confidence in one's own capacity to feel certain things. This should be the result.

December 23

> If I choose to bless another person, I will always feel that I have been blessed more than I did before.

Do something kind for other people whenever you're feeling sorry for yourself or full of self-loathing. This will force you out of your own head and into the world. When you were a kid, there was nothing more exciting than ripping through the wrapping paper on your birthday or Christmas presents. But as you get older, you come to understand that the best gift of all is the ability to bring a smile to the face of another person.

The purpose of this is to increase joy for as many people as possible by generously giving.

December 24

> Are you aware of the significance that the World of Pains and Troubles plays in the process of teaching an intelligence and providing it with a soul?

We come to this world so that we might experience every single feeling there is to feel. Because of this, we develop our bravery, compassion, and character. It has an effect on the people we are now as well as the people we will become in the future.

The goal is for you to think about or communicate with people in your life who you admire, and to inquire about the circumstances that influenced their lives.

December 25

> Visions and dreams are the progeny of your spirit and serve as the blueprints for your ultimate achievements; therefore, you should treasure them.

Since I was a little girl, I've had this burning desire to someday be a singer and performer. What I didn't realize as a youngster was that the dreams and goals that I started having at a young age were paving the way not just for my achievement but, more importantly, for my contentment.

This is something that I didn't discover until much later in life. I am so appreciative that, even when I was a small child, I paid attention to the feelings, dreams, and visions that came to me.

The goal is to remind people that it is never too late to live the life they have always desired, regardless of how old they are.

December 26

> I do not lack any sense of fear. I'm easily terrified. But I've also learned the skills I need to use that anger to make myself better.

My greatest obstacle has always been fear. In my lifetime, I have a huge list of goals and aspirations. Fear is an emotion that serves no purpose for me or anyone else on this earth; all it does is prevent us from getting things done.

The goal for today is to confront and triumph over one of your anxieties.

December 27

> When your heart is broken, I don't think anyone can offer you any sound advice.

No matter what anyone else says, the only thing that can help you feel better once your heart has been broken is the passage of time and the passage of distance. We are unable to recover from emotional trauma without the love and support of our family and friends, but there are times when no one can assist us.

There is a difference between feeling supported and feeling like someone is striving to fix you when you are going through difficult times. Realize that the most important thing you can do at this point is to let it take its natural course, regardless of whether it is your heart or the heart of someone else who has been broken.

The objective is to make an offer to cry on the shoulder of a friend or family member.

December 28

> Kindness is a universal language that may be understood by those who are hard of hearing or seeing.

There are no barriers to kindness, not even language, disease, or a handicap. Do not squander the opportunity because it is a human gift that can only be given and received by all people. The mission for the day is to show courtesy to a complete stranger.

December 29

> There is simply not enough time in this life for anyone to feel entitled to take any part of it for granted. There is a lot for which I should express gratitude right now.

At some points in our lives, it's easy to get caught up in dwelling on the things we lack. It is essential to remind oneself to practice gratitude for everything that one owns. When you focus on all the wonderful things that are already in your life, you will connect with the numerous blessings that you already have and attract even more of them. When I get up in the morning or before I go to bed at night, I'll sometimes sit down and create a list of everything I'm grateful for. Before I know it, I'll have pages of things on the list, and I'll be beaming with happiness and smiling broadly. This month, consider contributing to a nonprofit organization or volunteering some of your time to assist others who are less fortunate than you.

December 30

> Everyone was given a specific mission when they were created, and the desire to fulfill that mission has been instilled in the hearts of all people.

At some point in our lives, each of us has pondered the question, "Where am I?" There are times when we need to experience what it's like to be disoriented in order to fully understand and know where we want to go. Whatever it is that you are experiencing, try to keep in mind that each and every one of us has been placed on this earth with a reason and a goal in mind. Our one and only duty is to acknowledge this and act in accordance with it. You shouldn't beat yourself up too much if you still haven't acknowledged it. Keep an open mind and be grateful for whatever opportunities present themselves to you as you put your faith in the universe to provide for you at the appropriate moment.

Take your time and aimlessly roam around while you're feeling disoriented. You are going to have to settle on a choice at some point in time.

December 31

The desire to be perfect is overpowered by the feeling of being loved.

You shouldn't worry about being perfect all the time. Invest your time and energy in ensuring that you spend the majority of your life not only giving but also receiving love. Nobody will remember you for the ways in which you were flawed; rather, people will remember you for the ways in which you were kind, humorous, and compassionate. Put an end to pretending that you are perfect and start appreciating life more.

MESSAGE I HAVE FOR YOU

For the sole purpose of simplifying the lives of my readers, I have devoted a significant amount of my time and effort to producing all of this high-quality content.

Since I do this from the heart and it is the only real goal I have set for myself, if I am able to help you take even a few small steps forward, in the direction of positivity and fulfillment, I will feel great satisfaction.

I take this opportunity to sincerely thank each of you for taking the time to read what I have written.

I have no doubt that by providing a positive assessment of my work, you will help promote the encouraging character of my publications. I thank you in advance for your help in this endeavor.

Likewise, I am sincerely grateful to you.

Other title published by

Imani Williams

EMOTIONAL SELF-CARE

for

Black Women

A Year of Strong Positive Affirmations for Modern Black Women and BIPOCs: Better Yourself, Retrain Your Mind, and Silence Your Inner Critic by Raising Self-Esteem!